I am grateful to God for everything! And I believe that the meaning of life is to give meaning to other lives. I dedicate this book to my family and to all the children in the world who love Nature. Life surprise me!!!

Mica Silva
2024

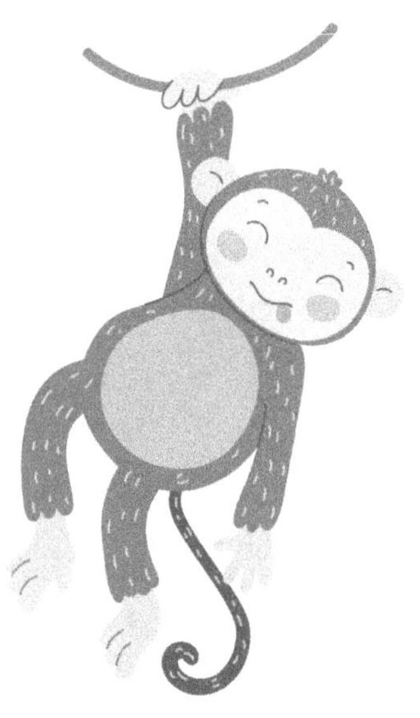
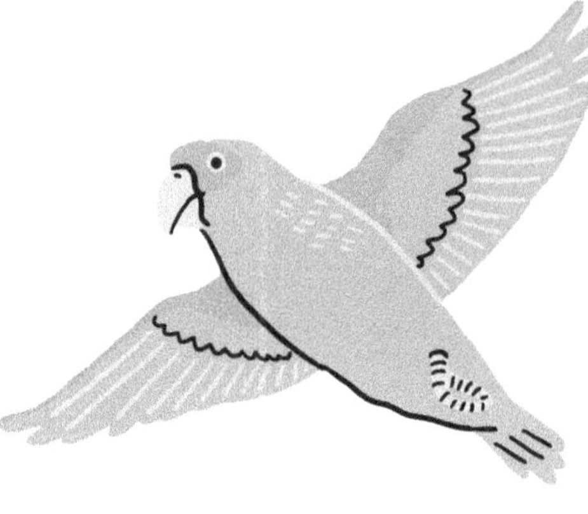

This Book Belongs to:

____

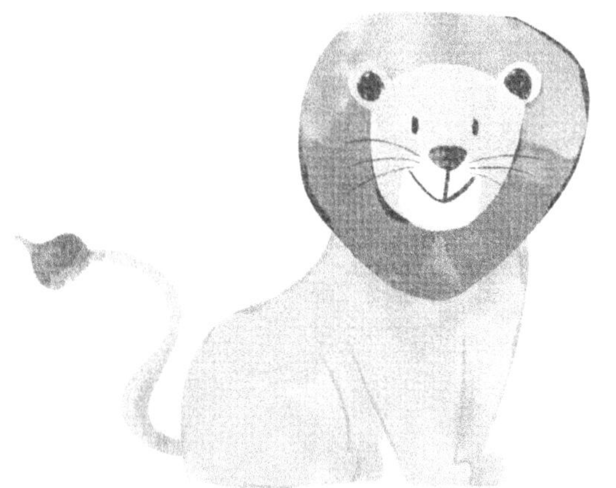
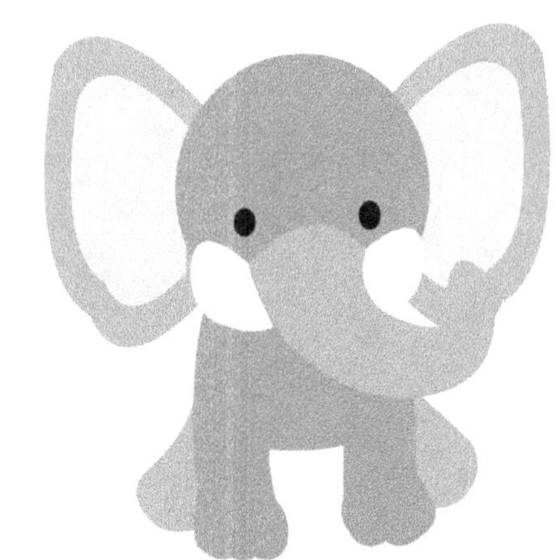

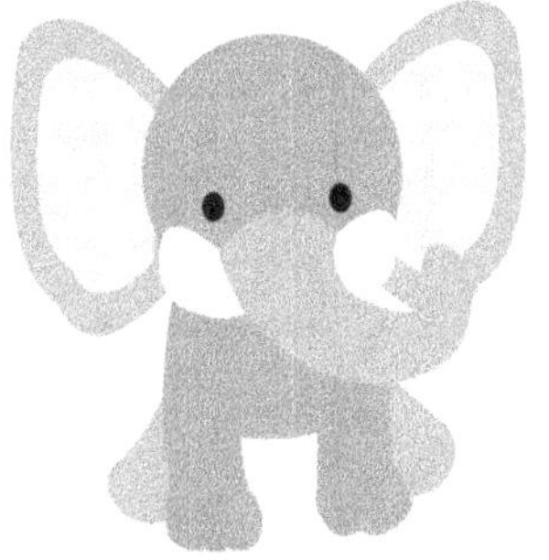

Test Color Page

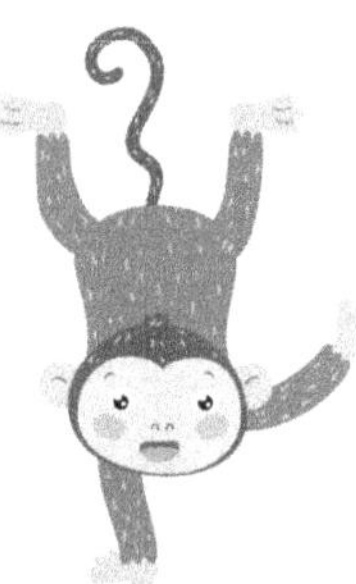

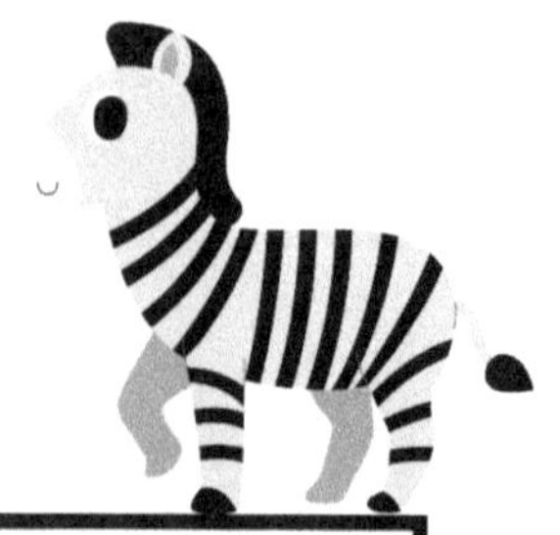

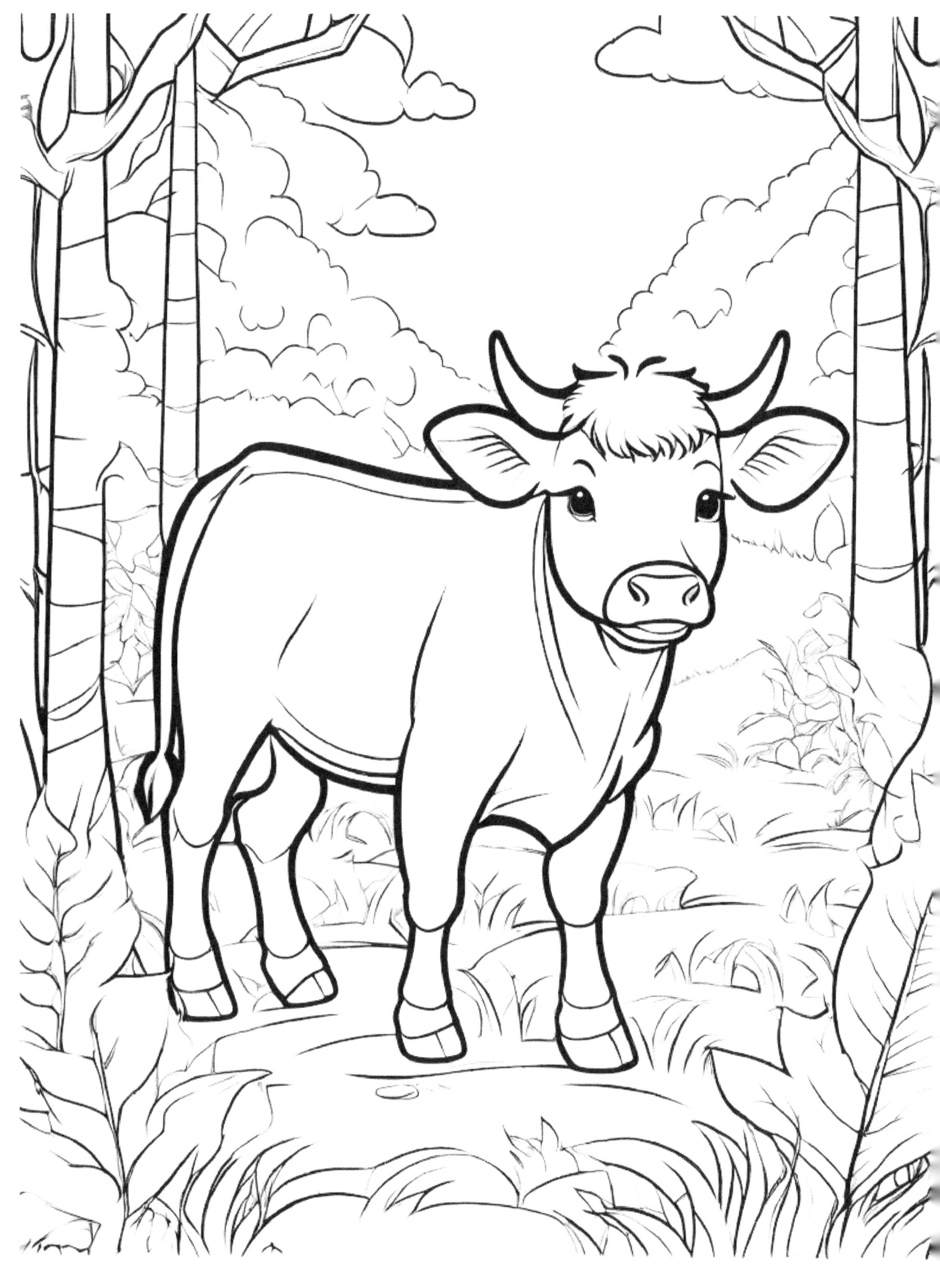

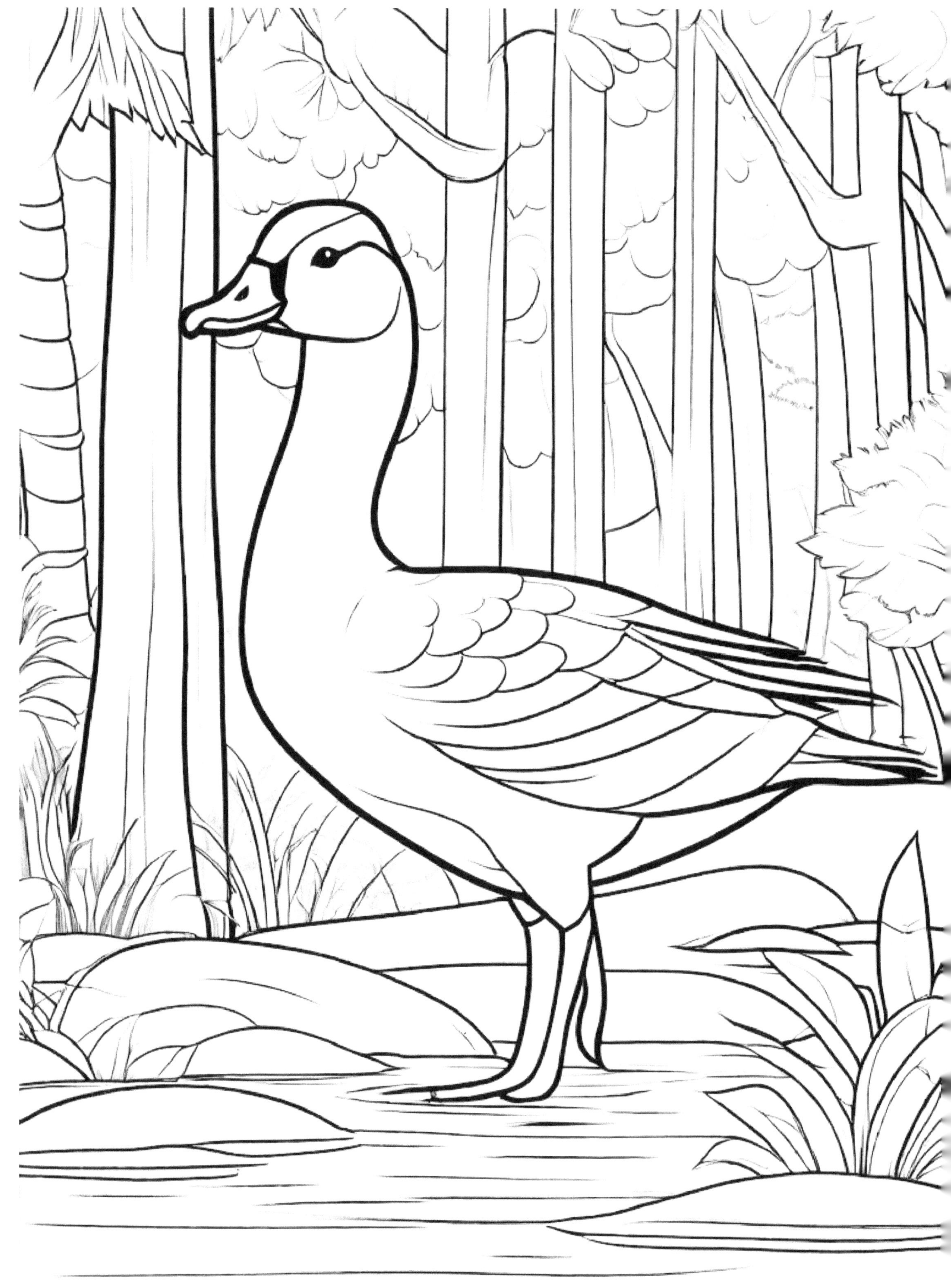

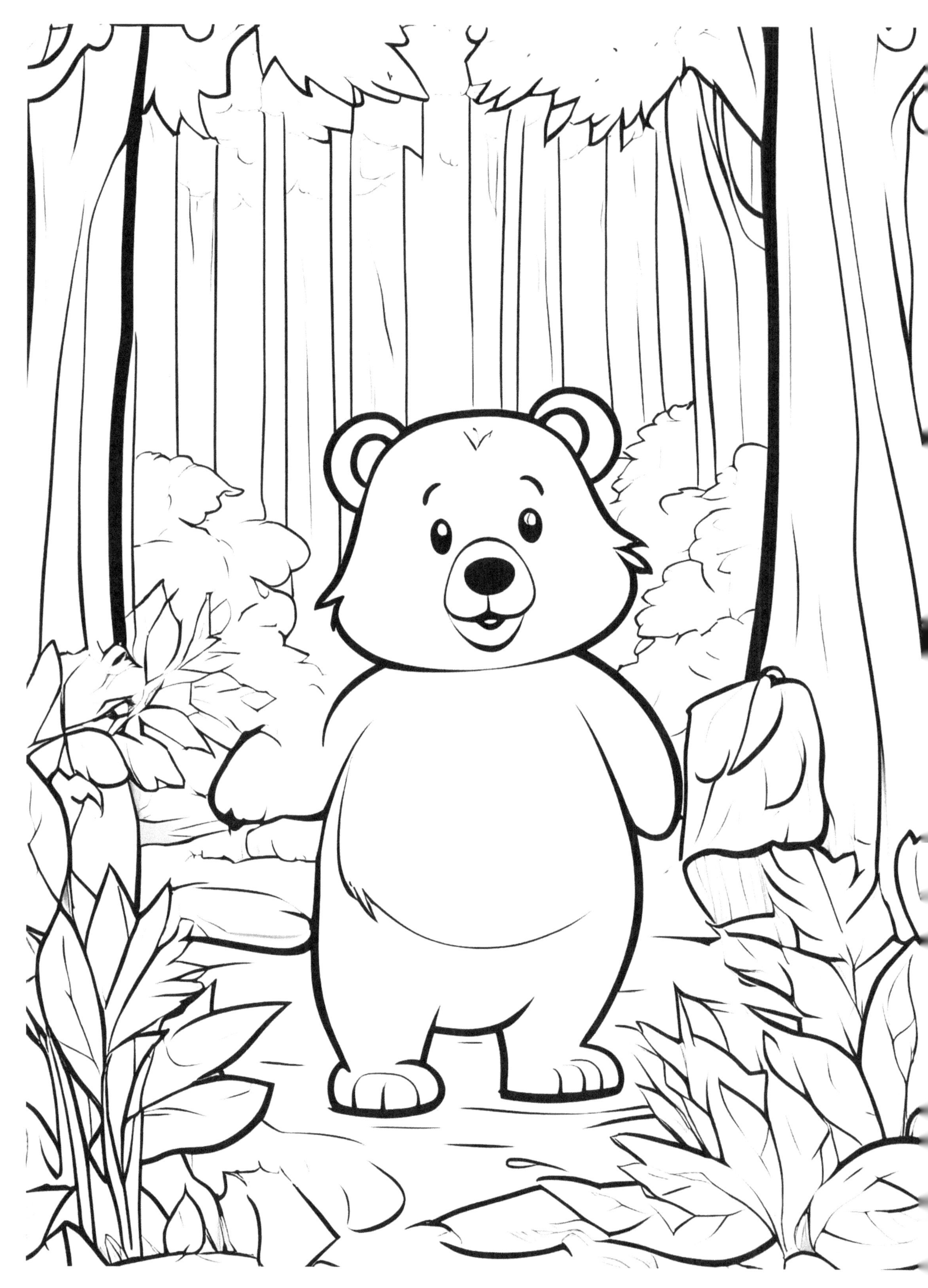

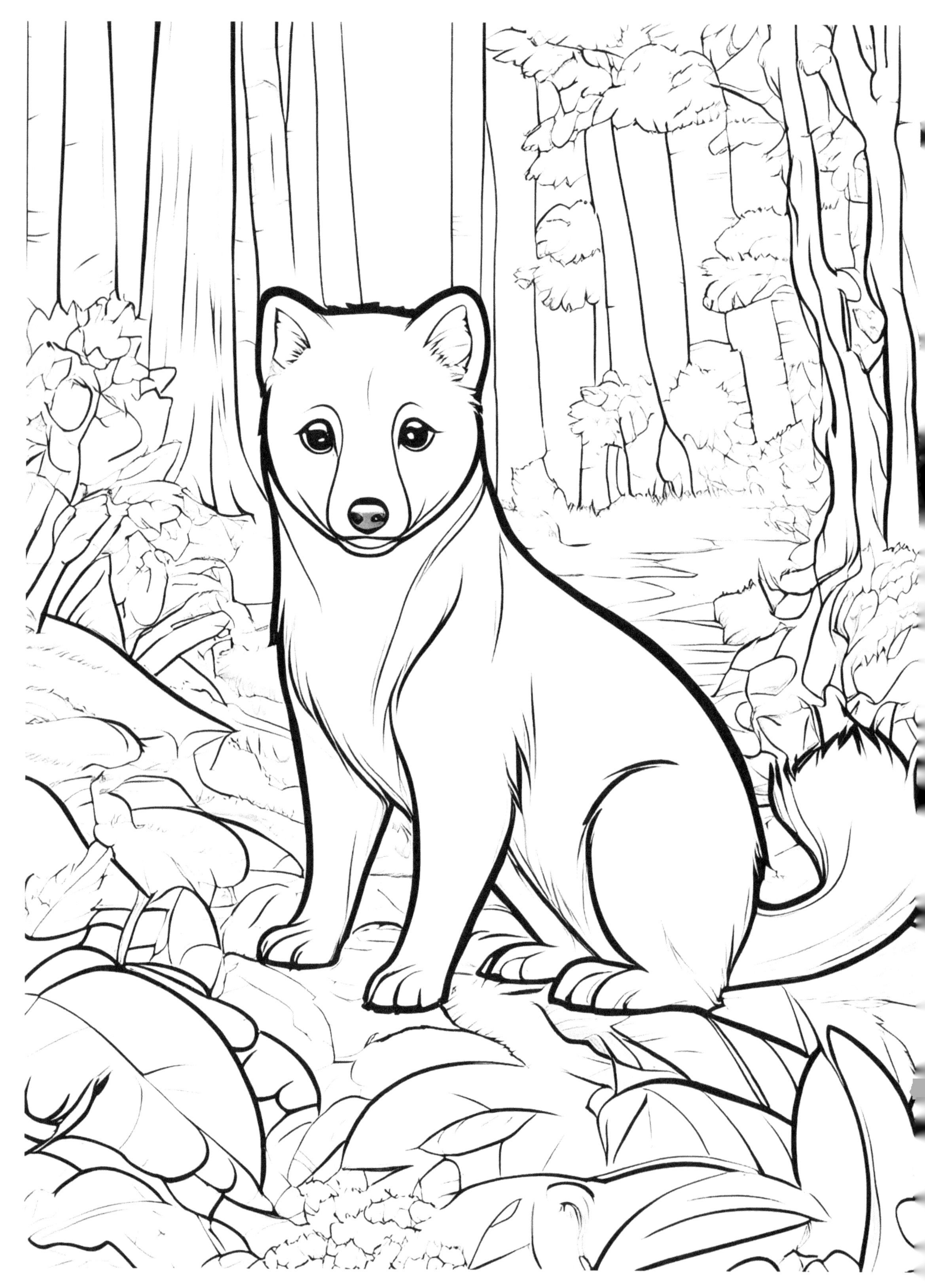

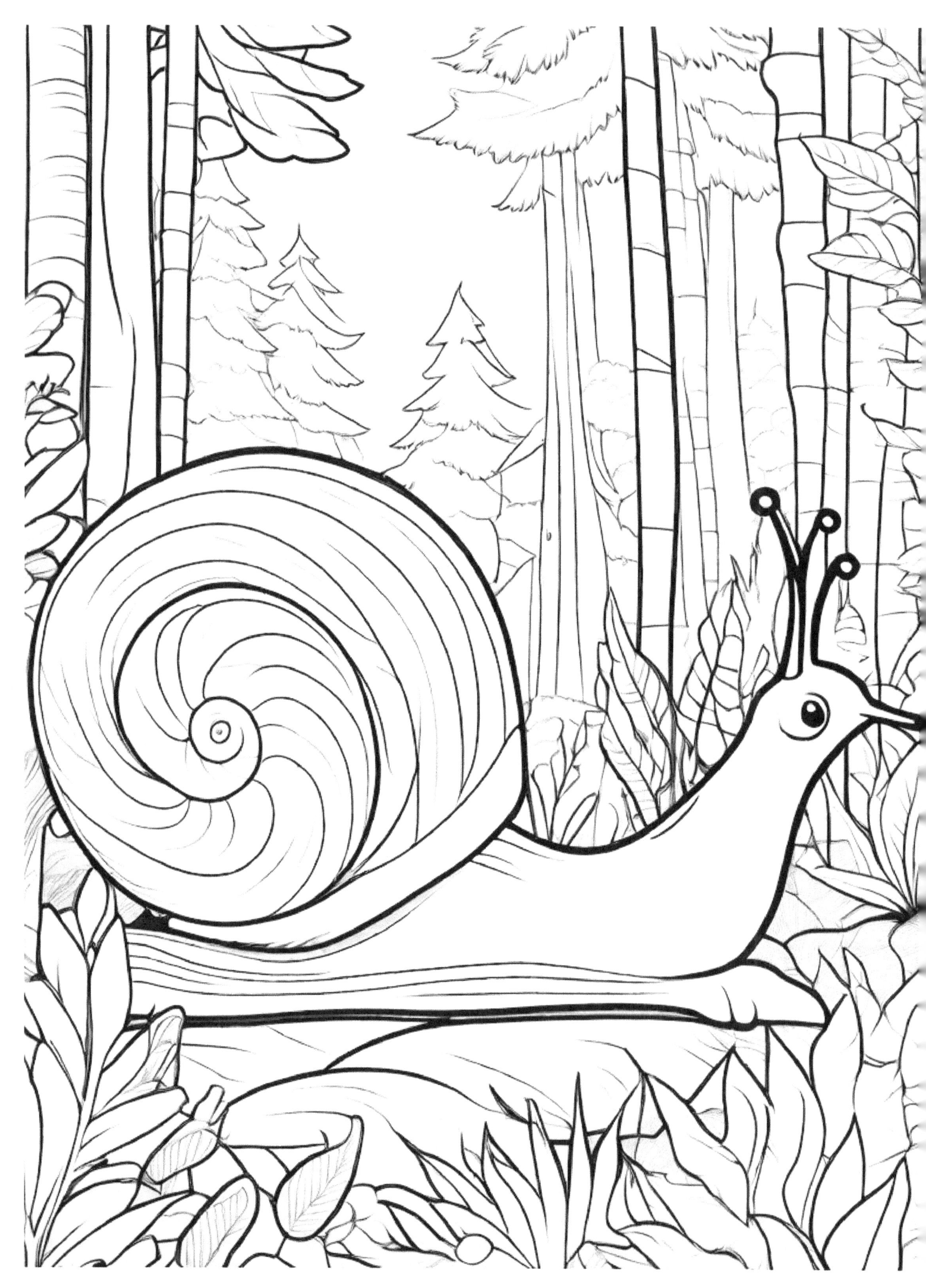

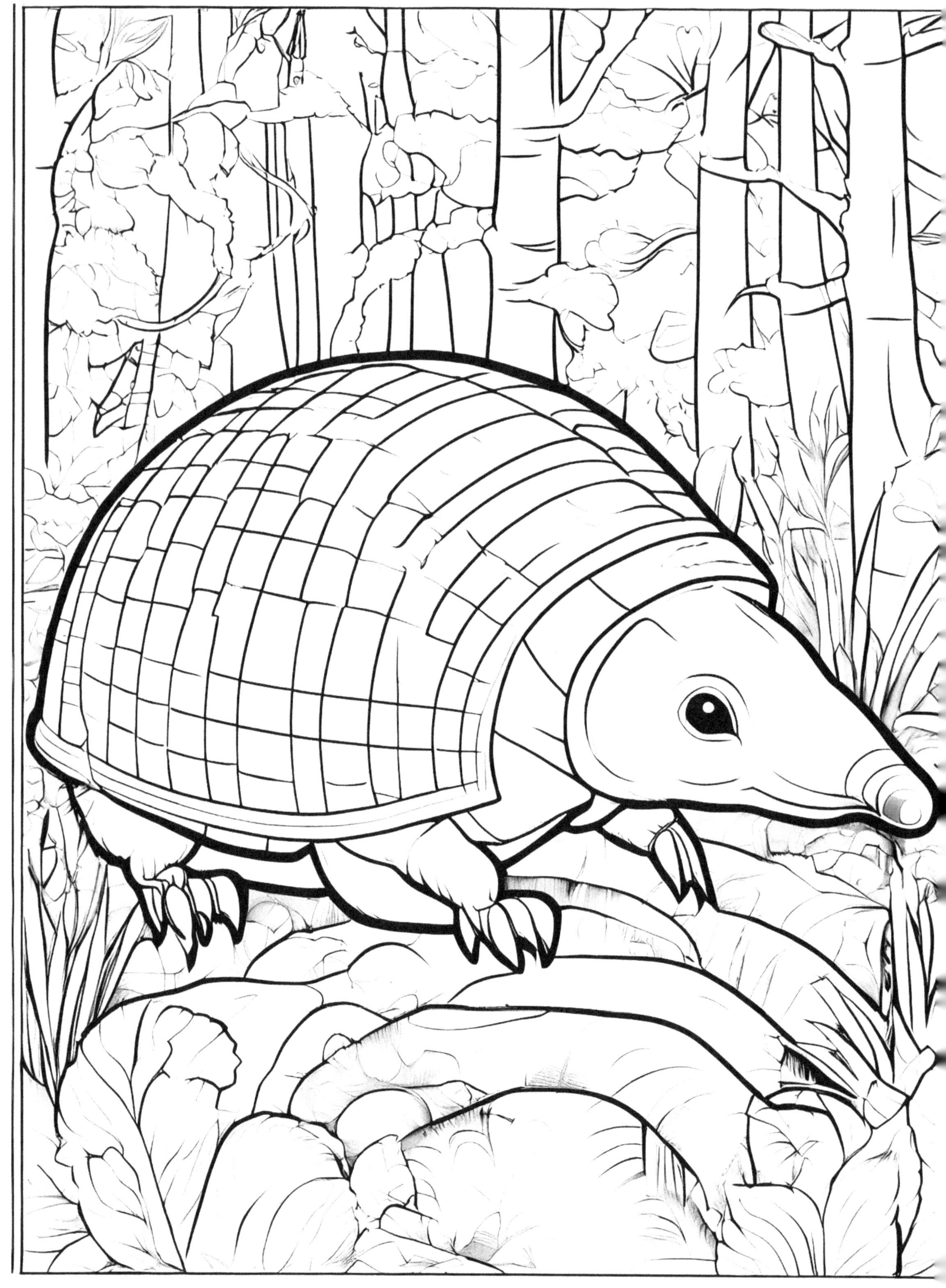

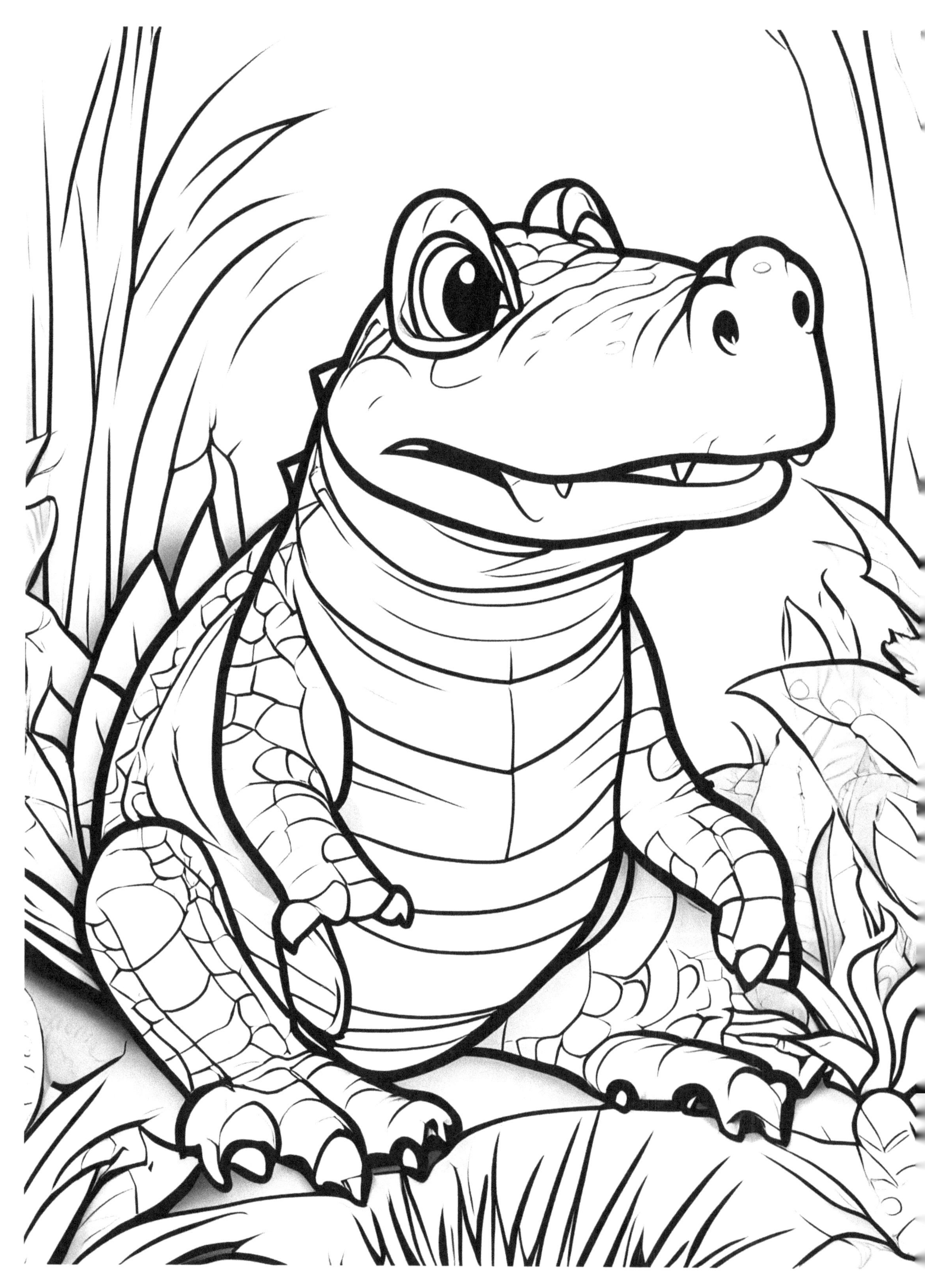

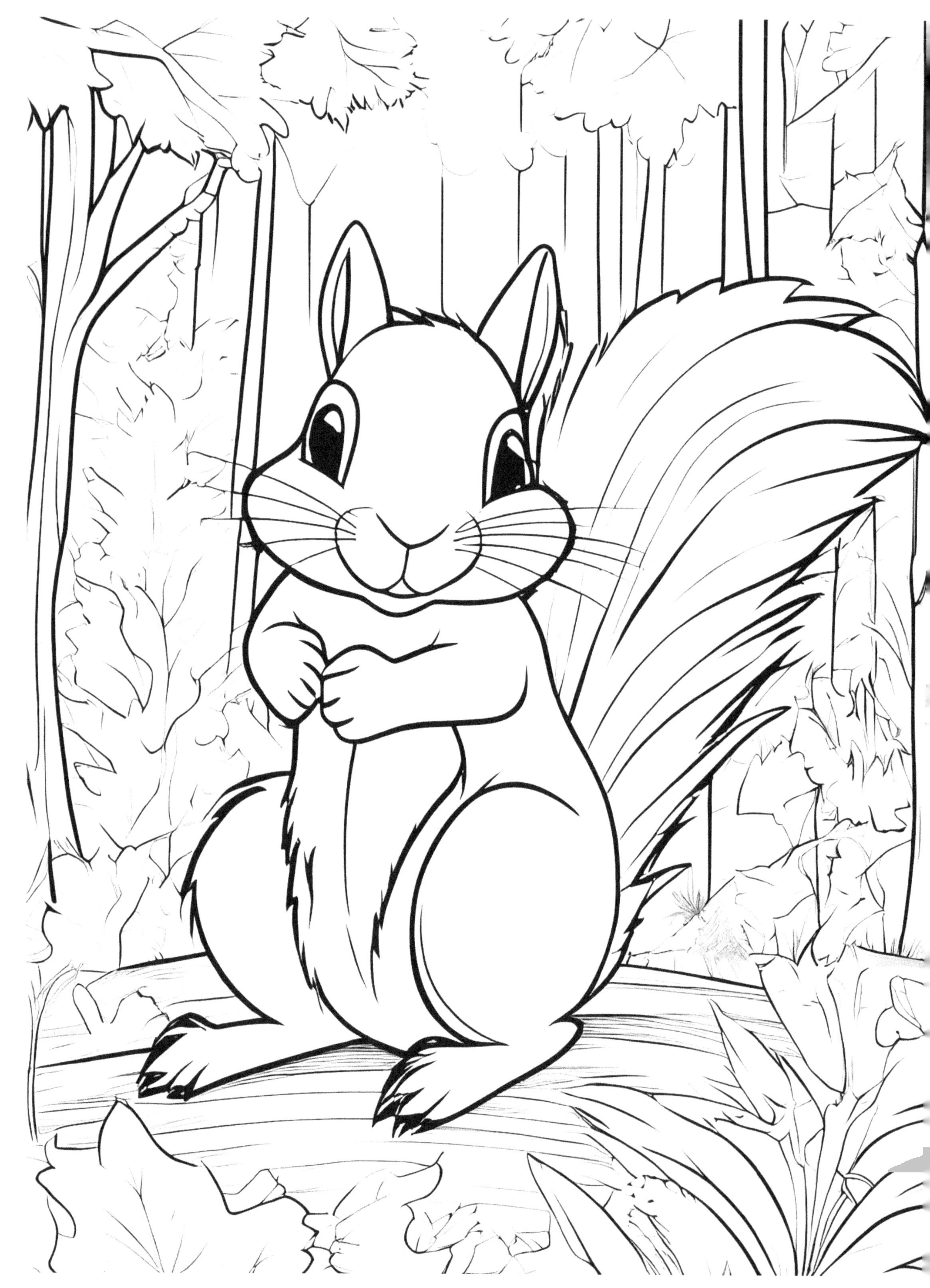

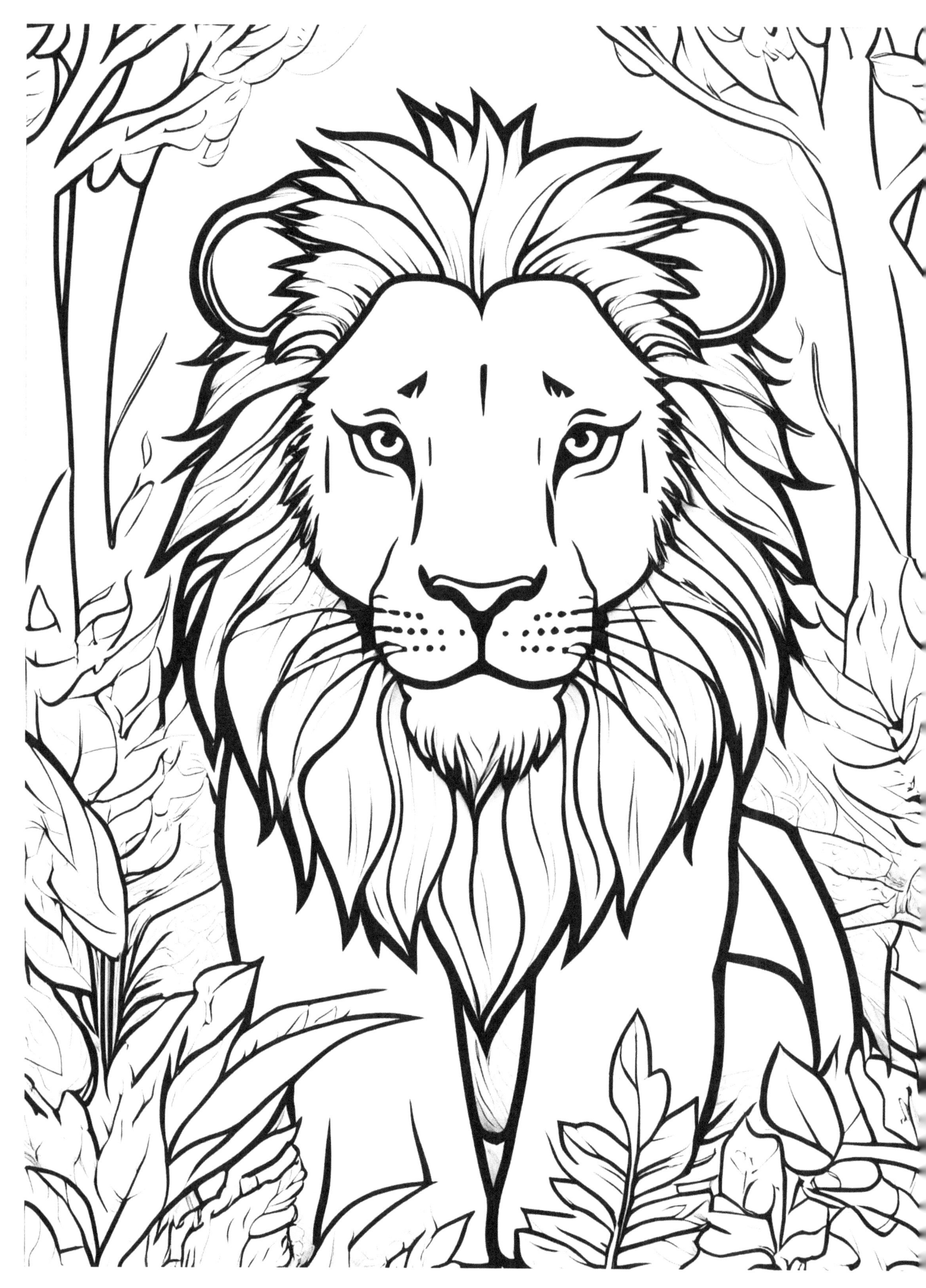

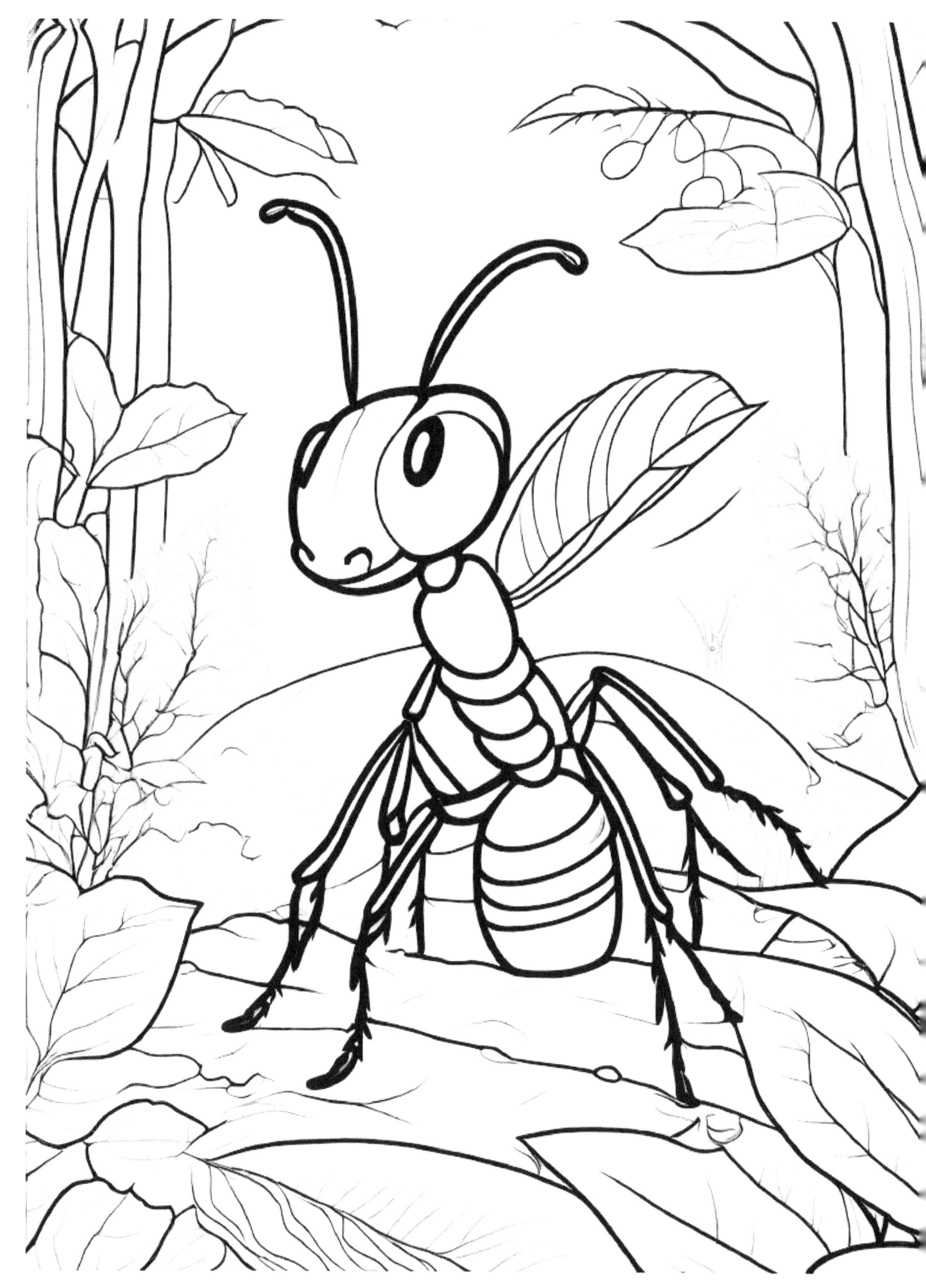

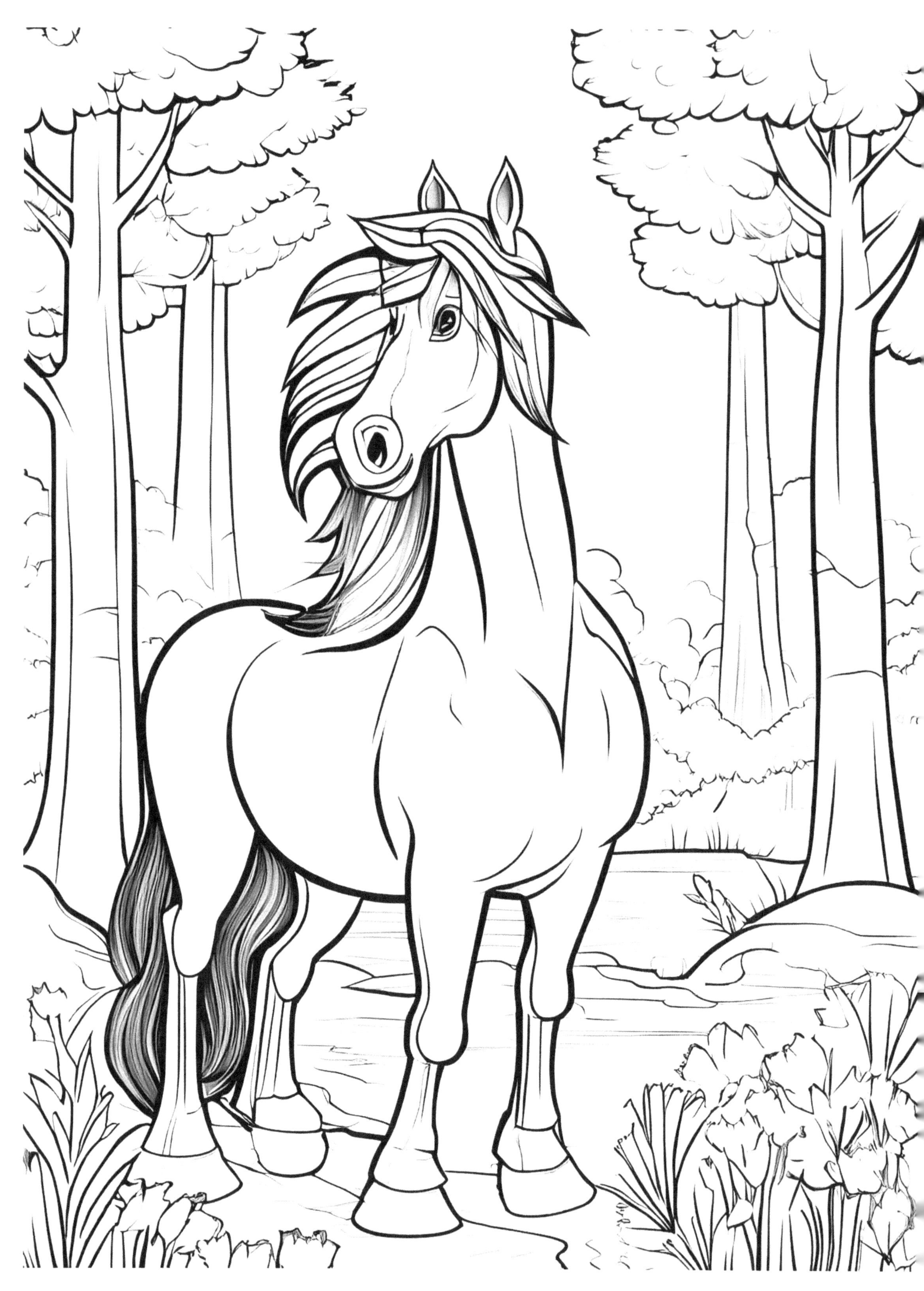

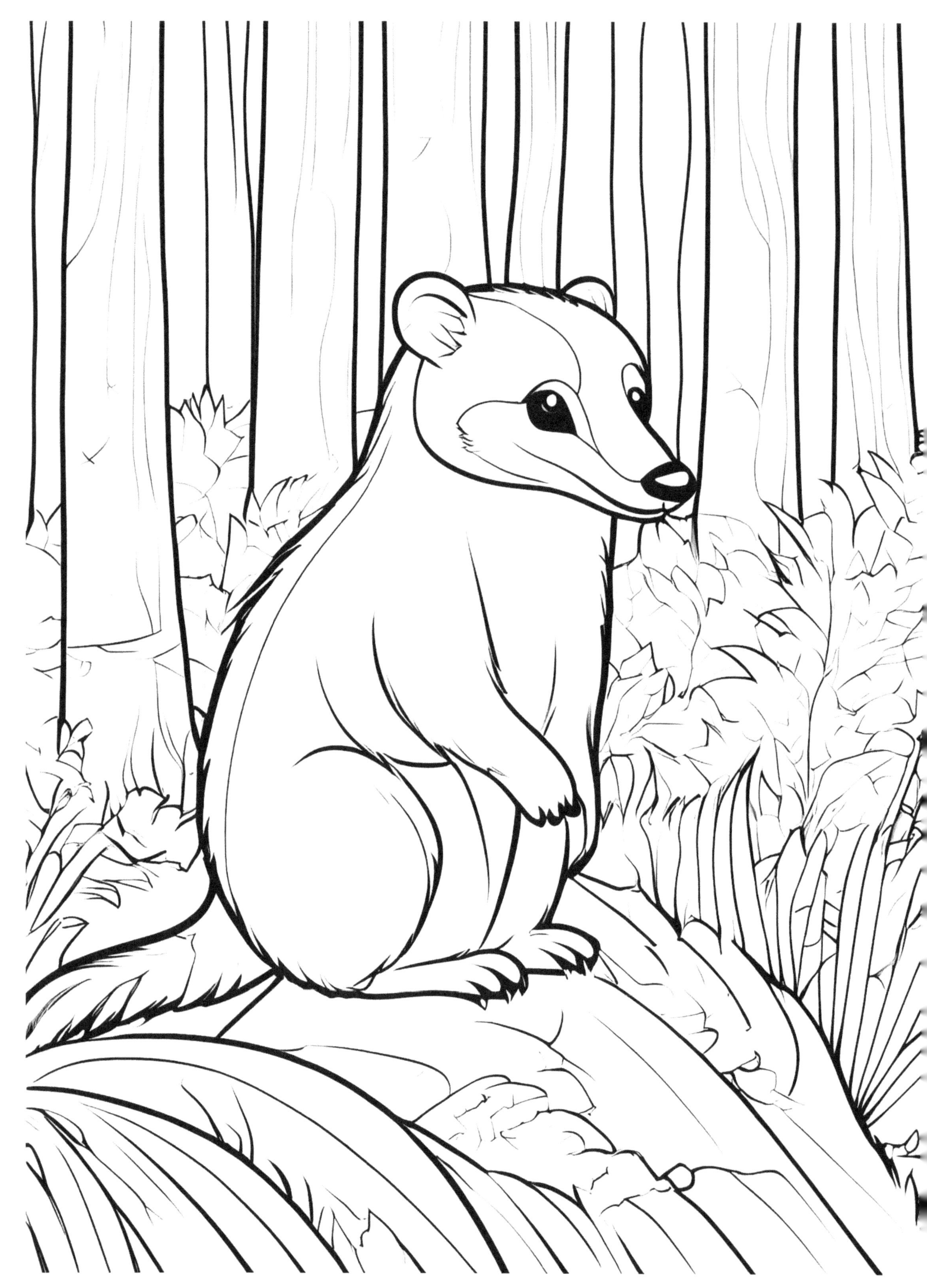

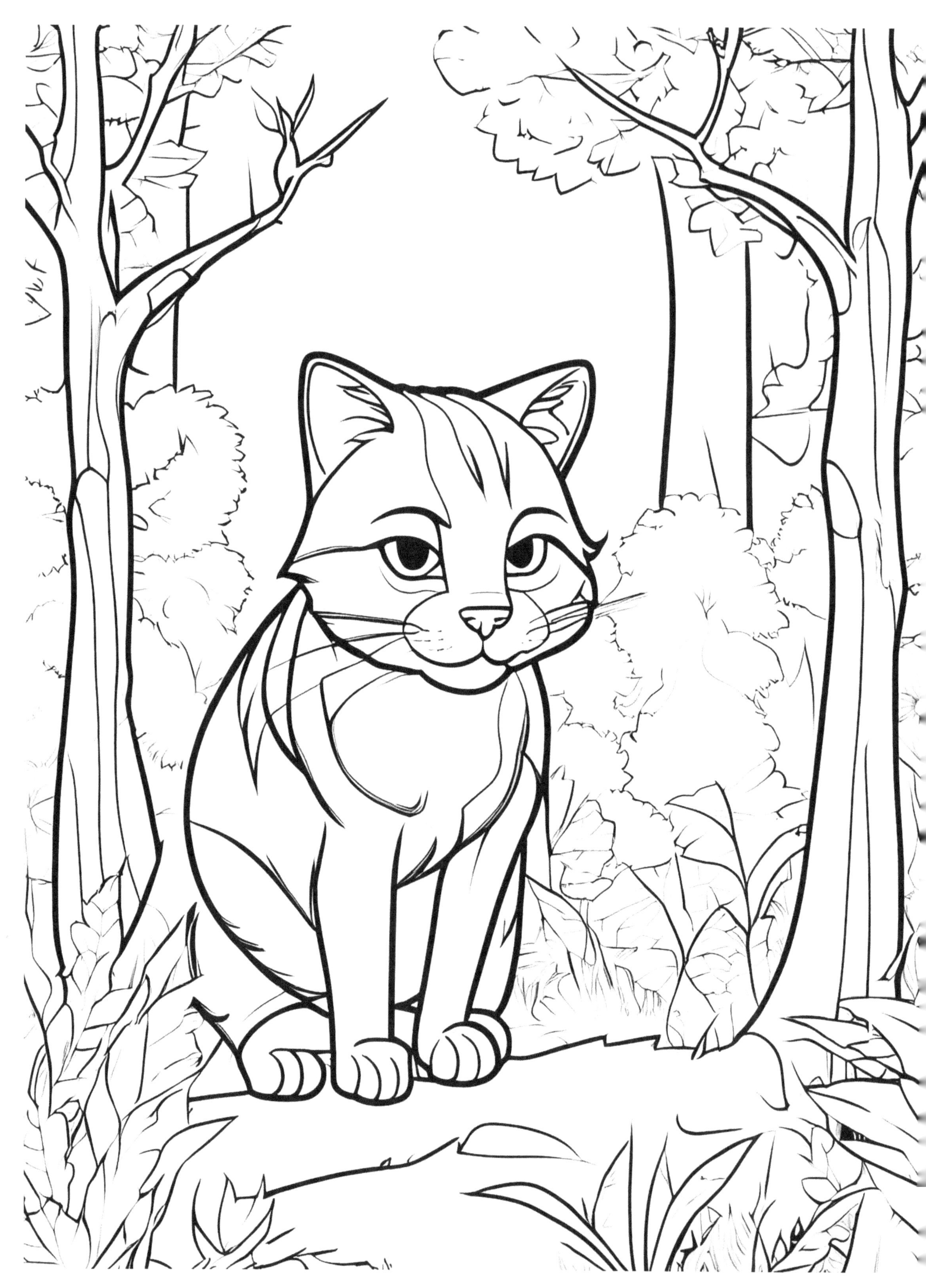

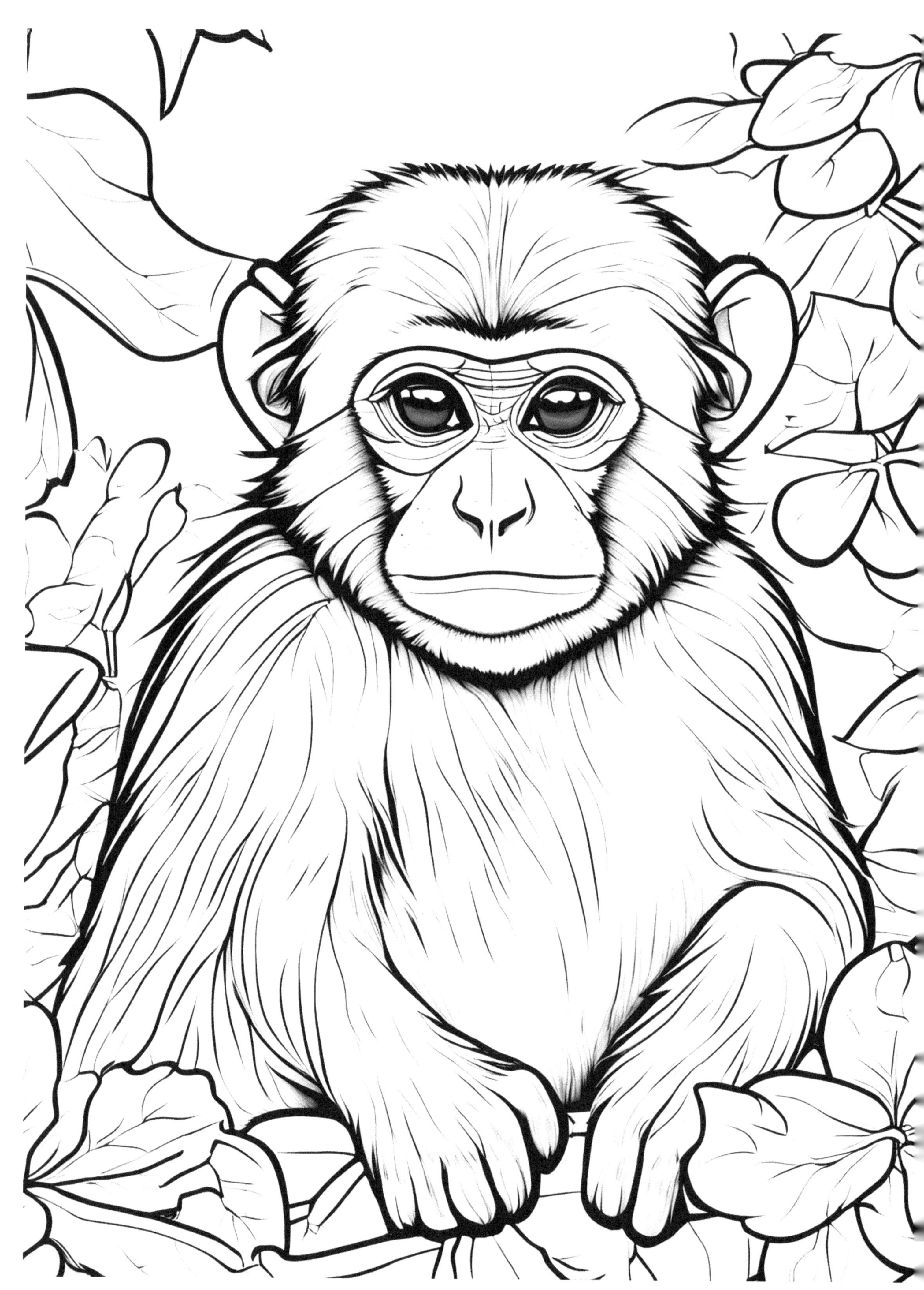

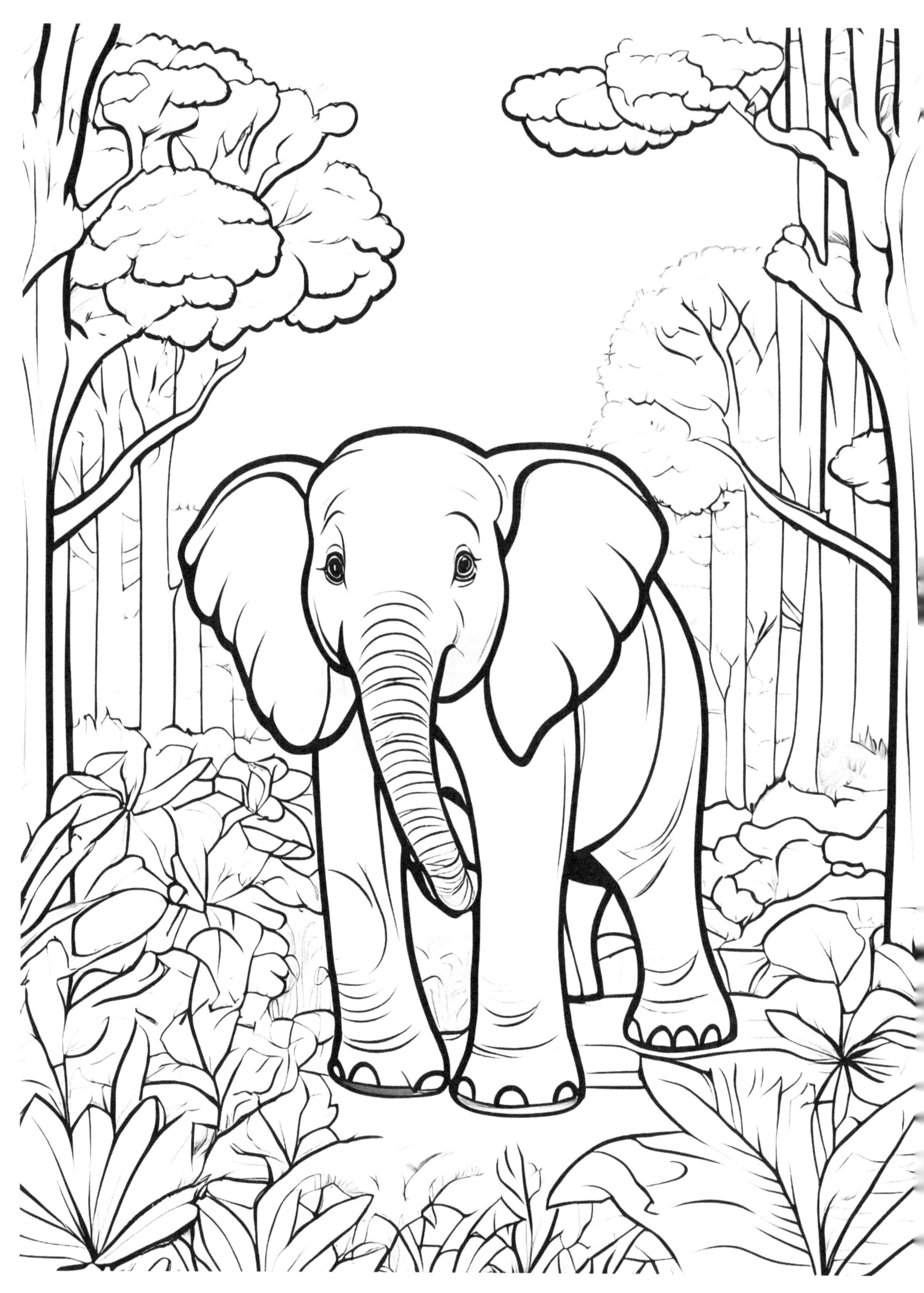

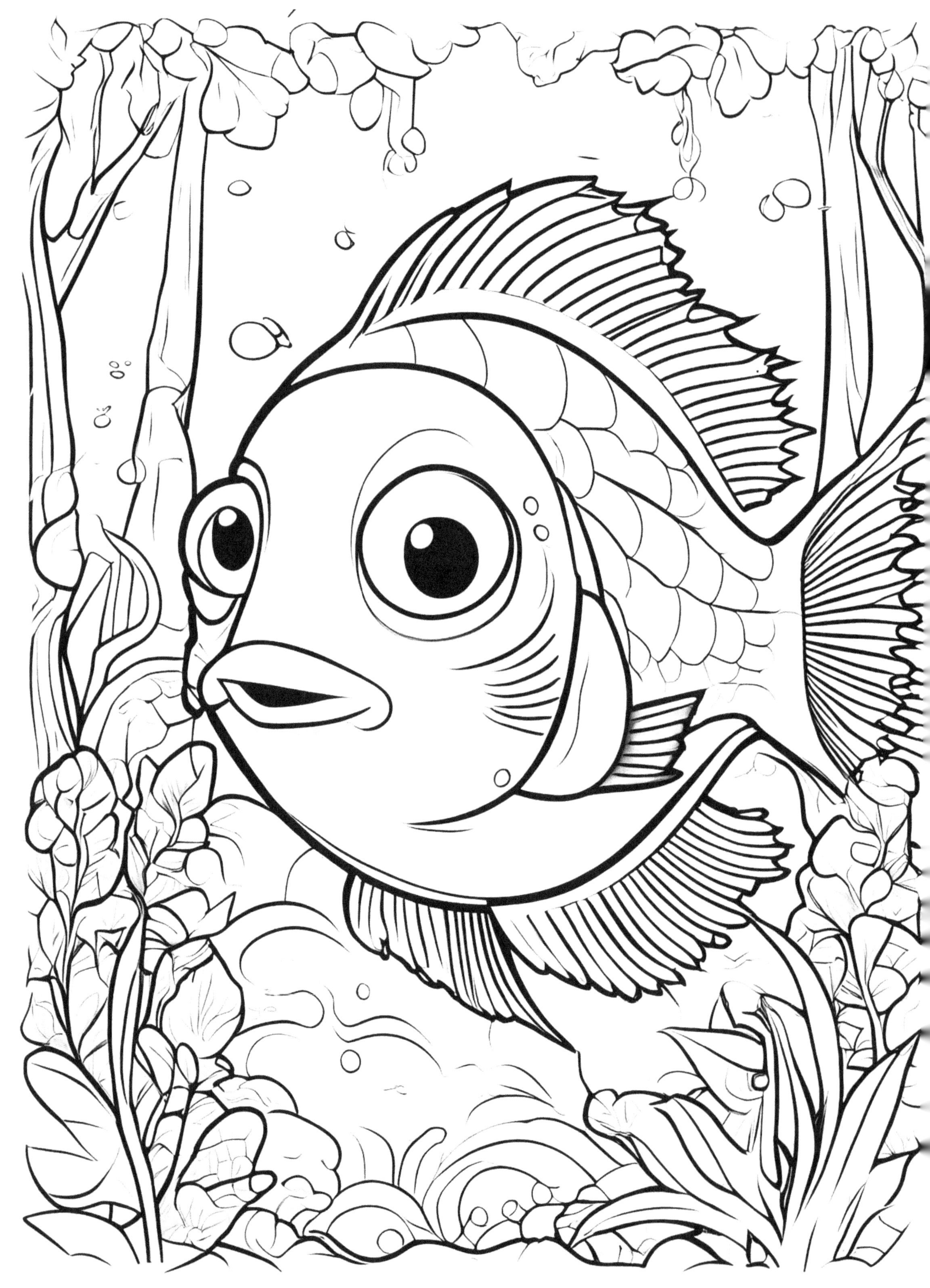

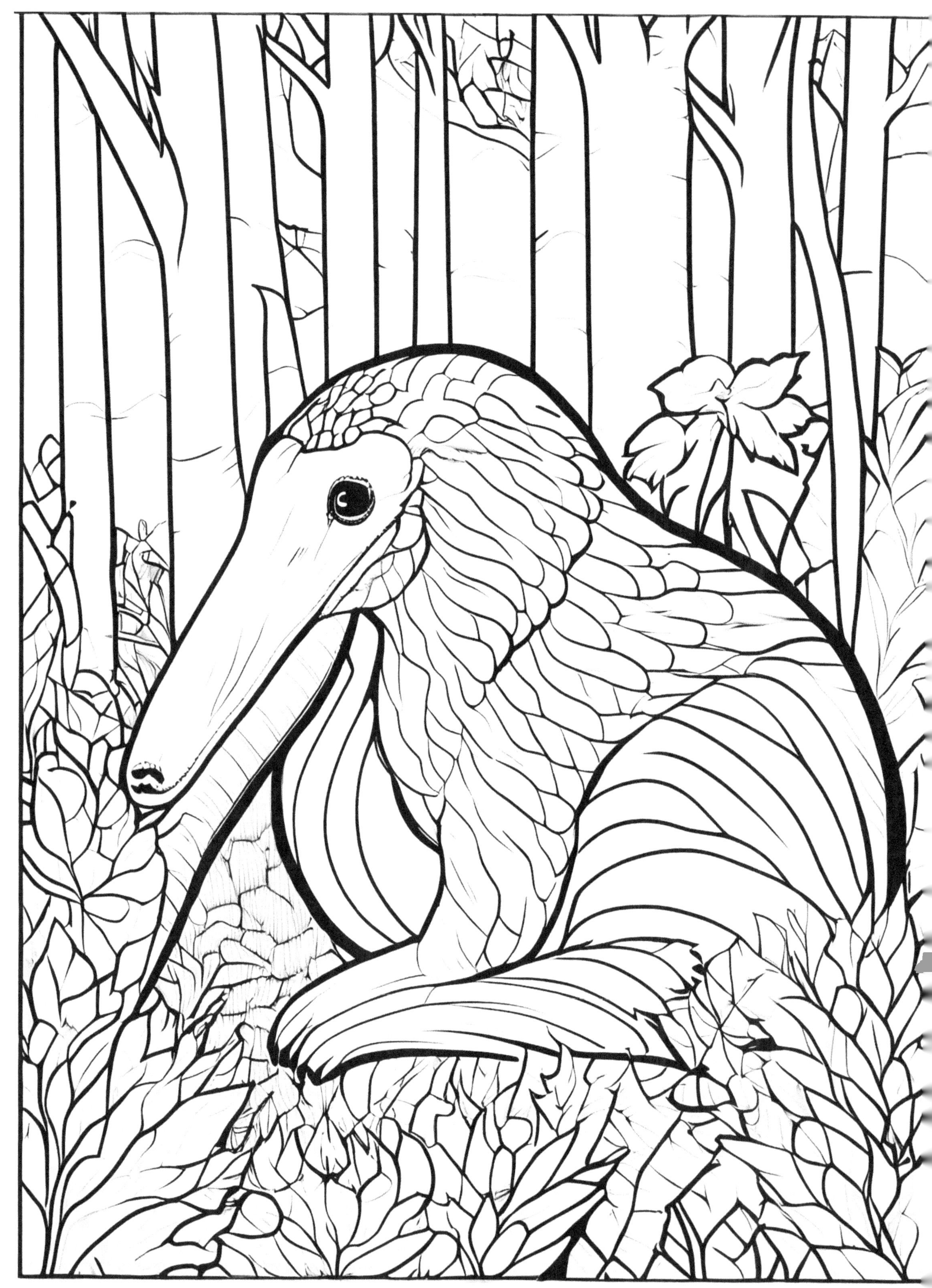

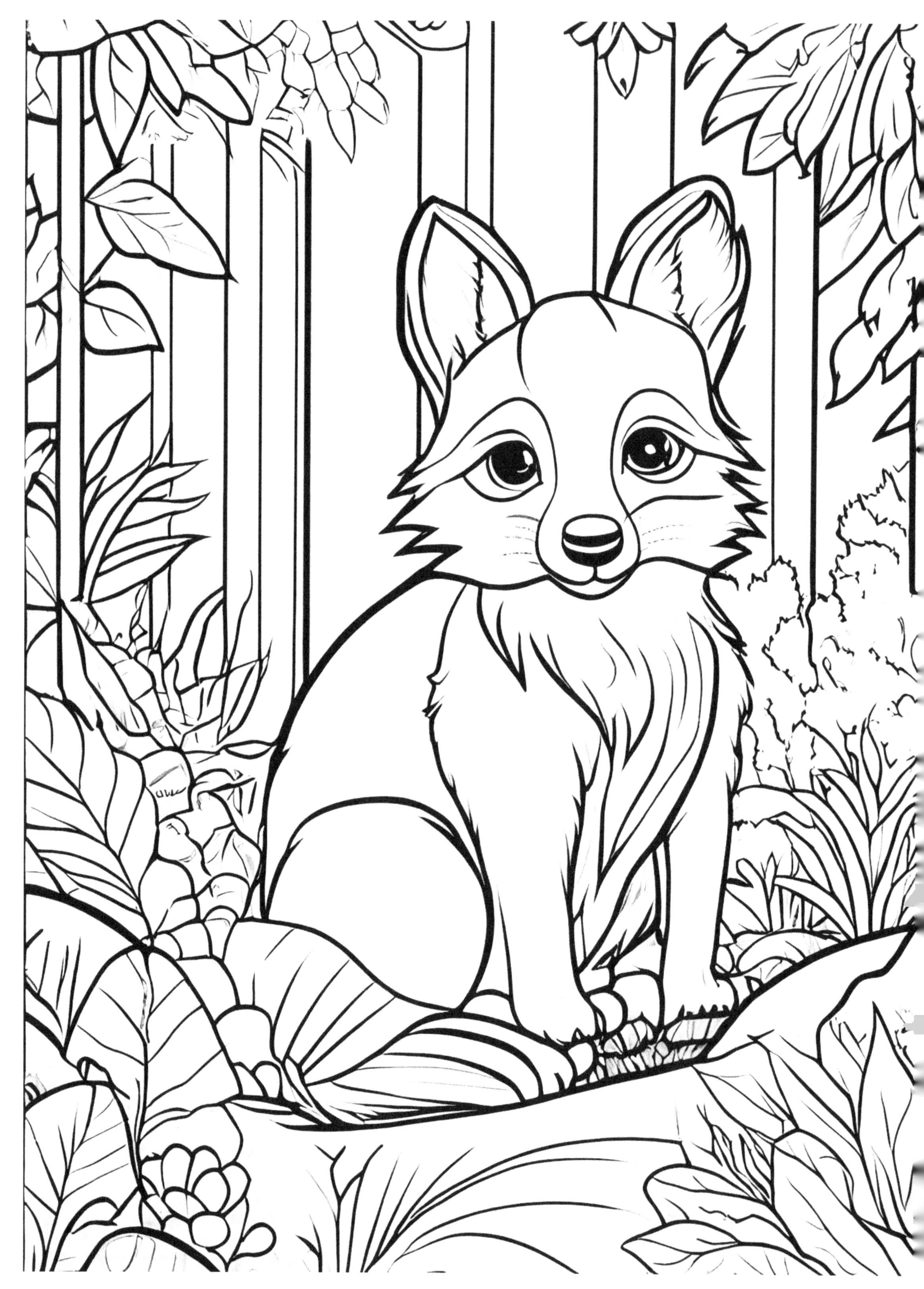

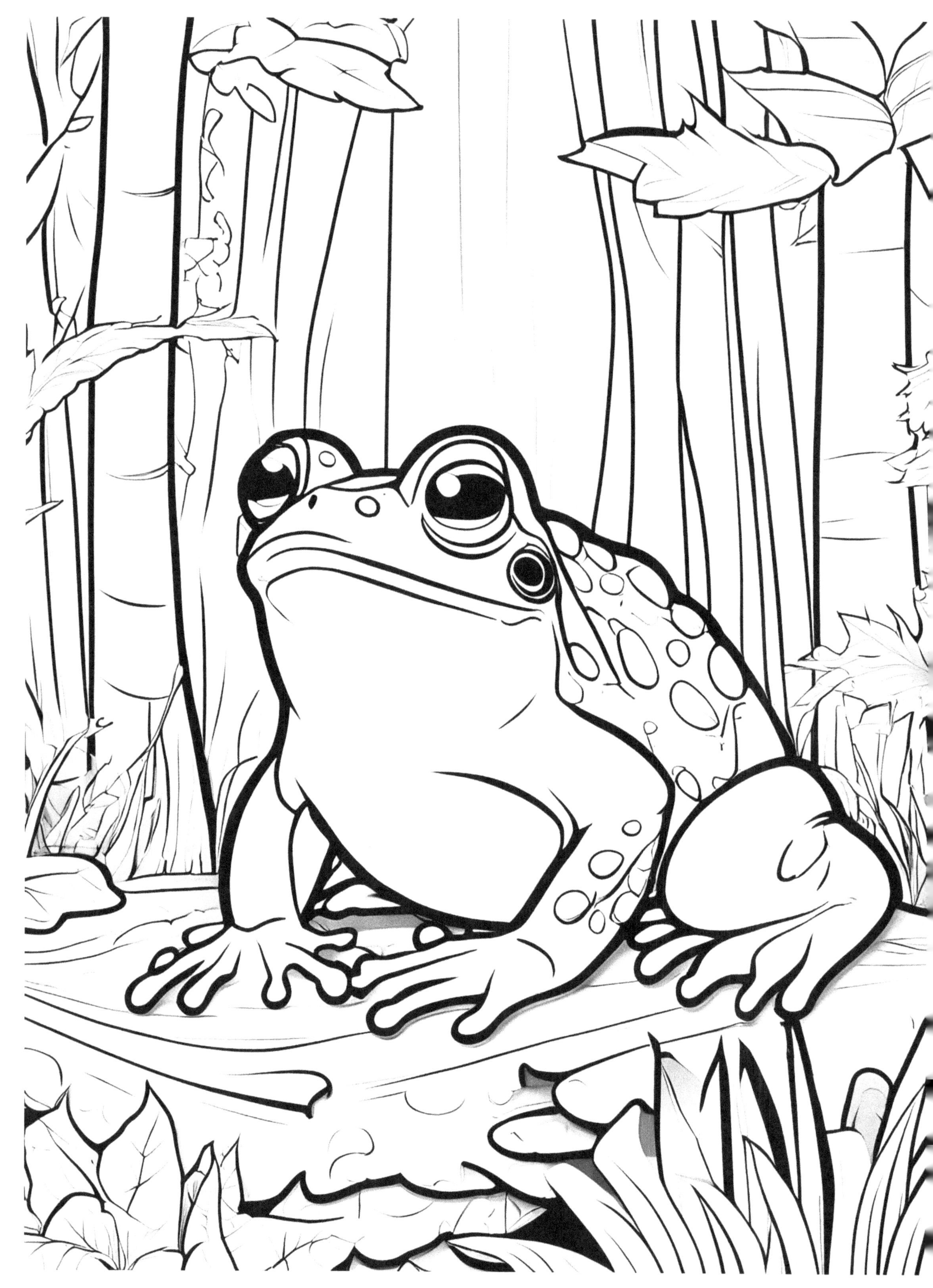

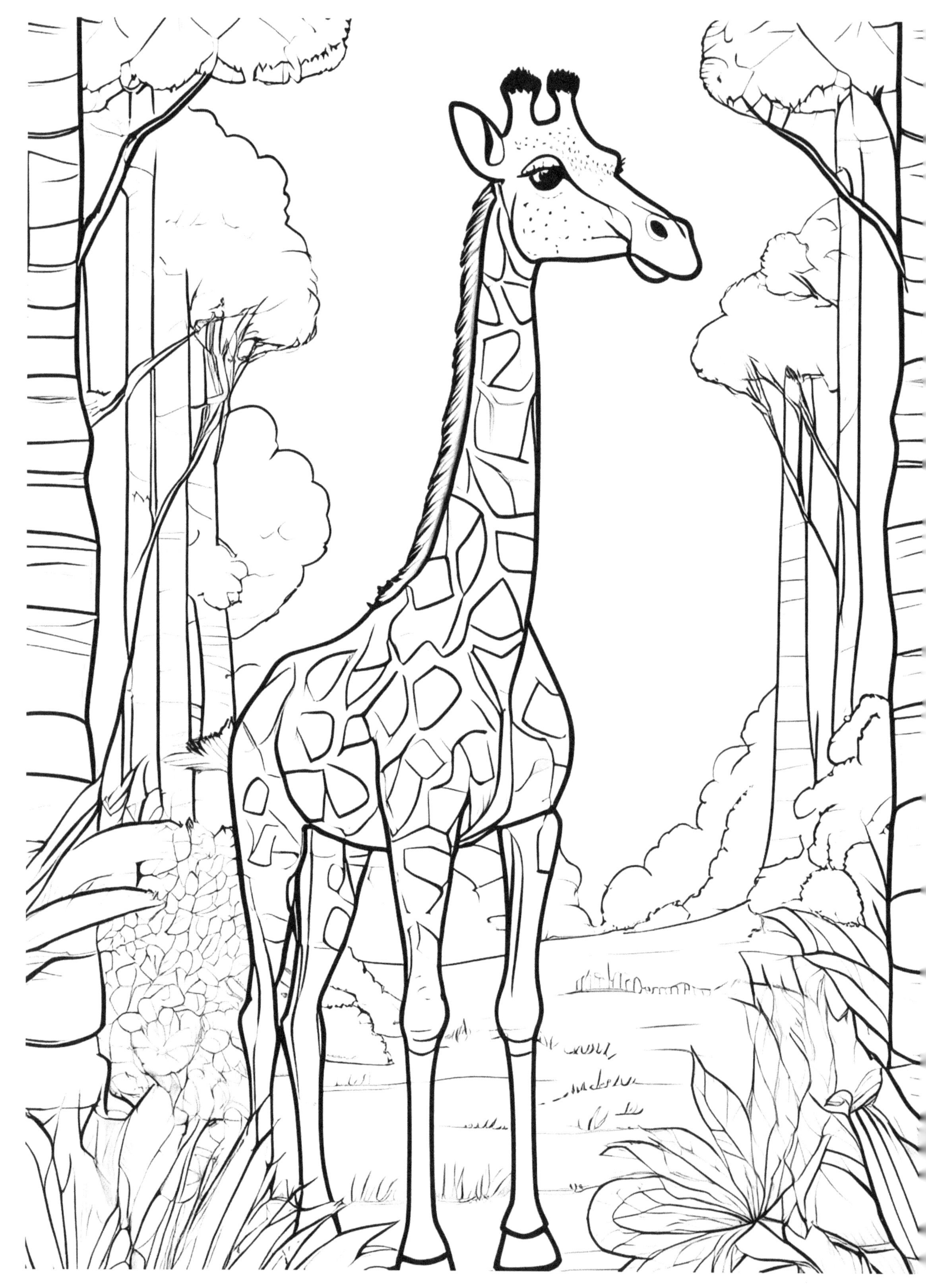

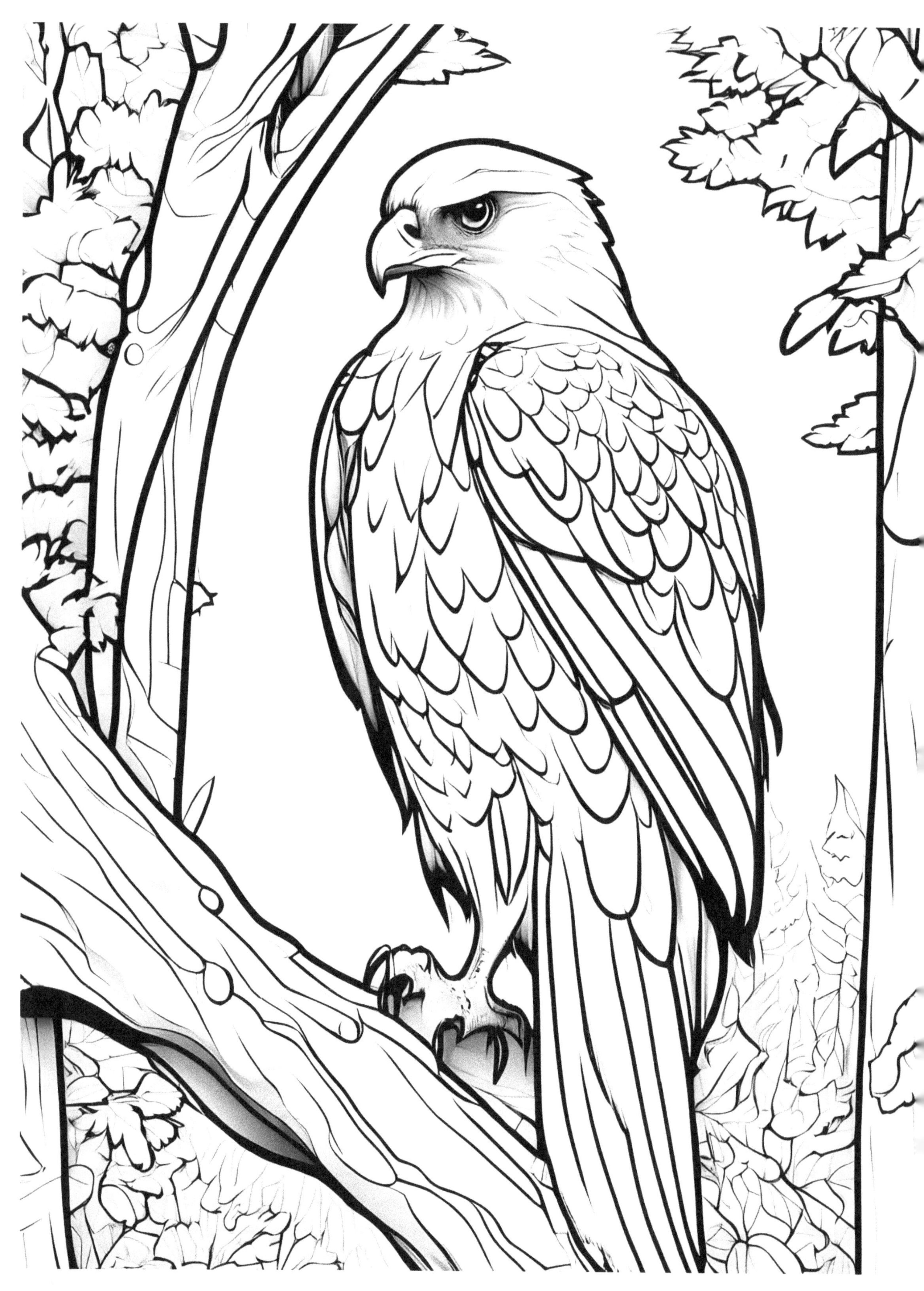

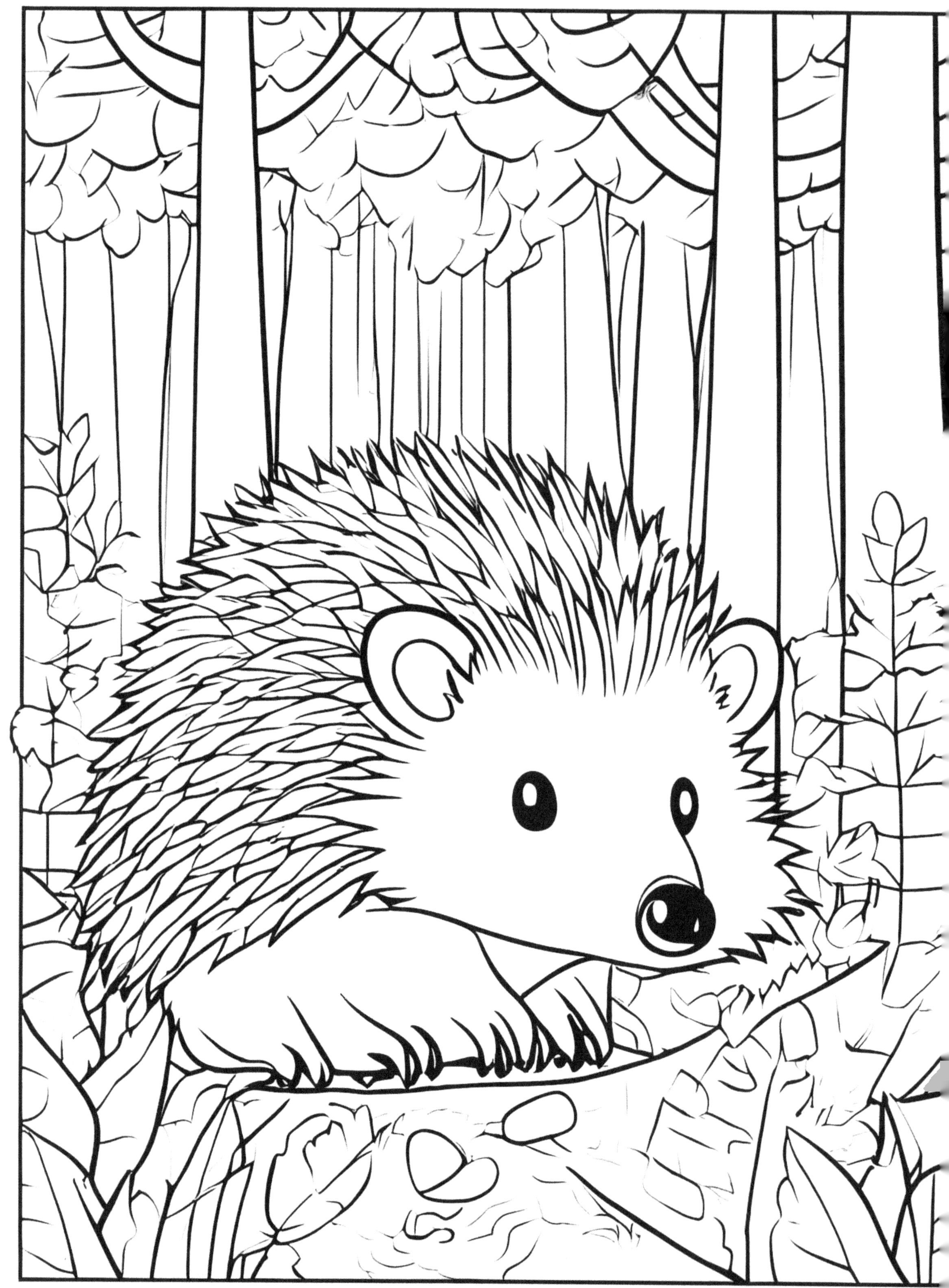

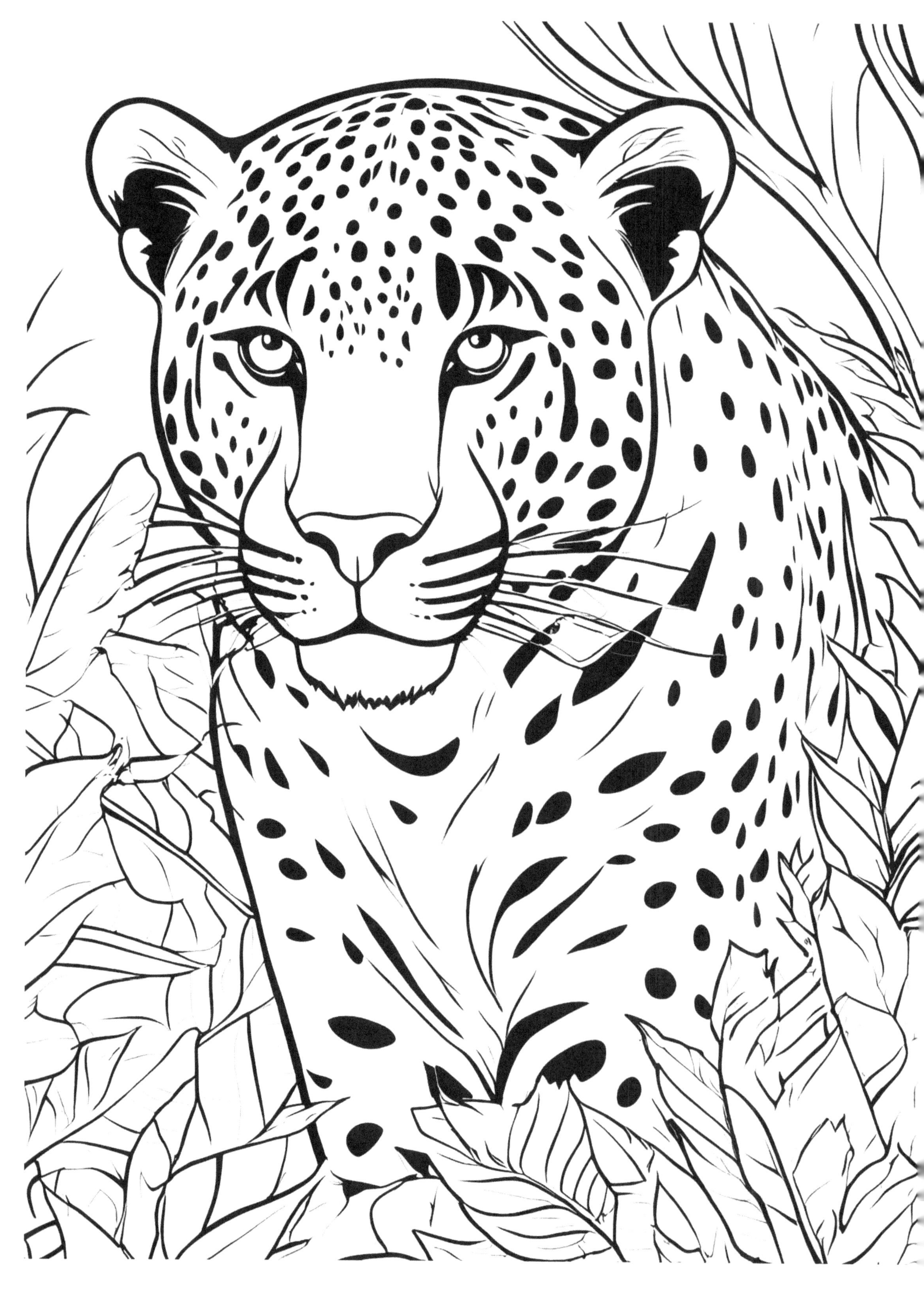

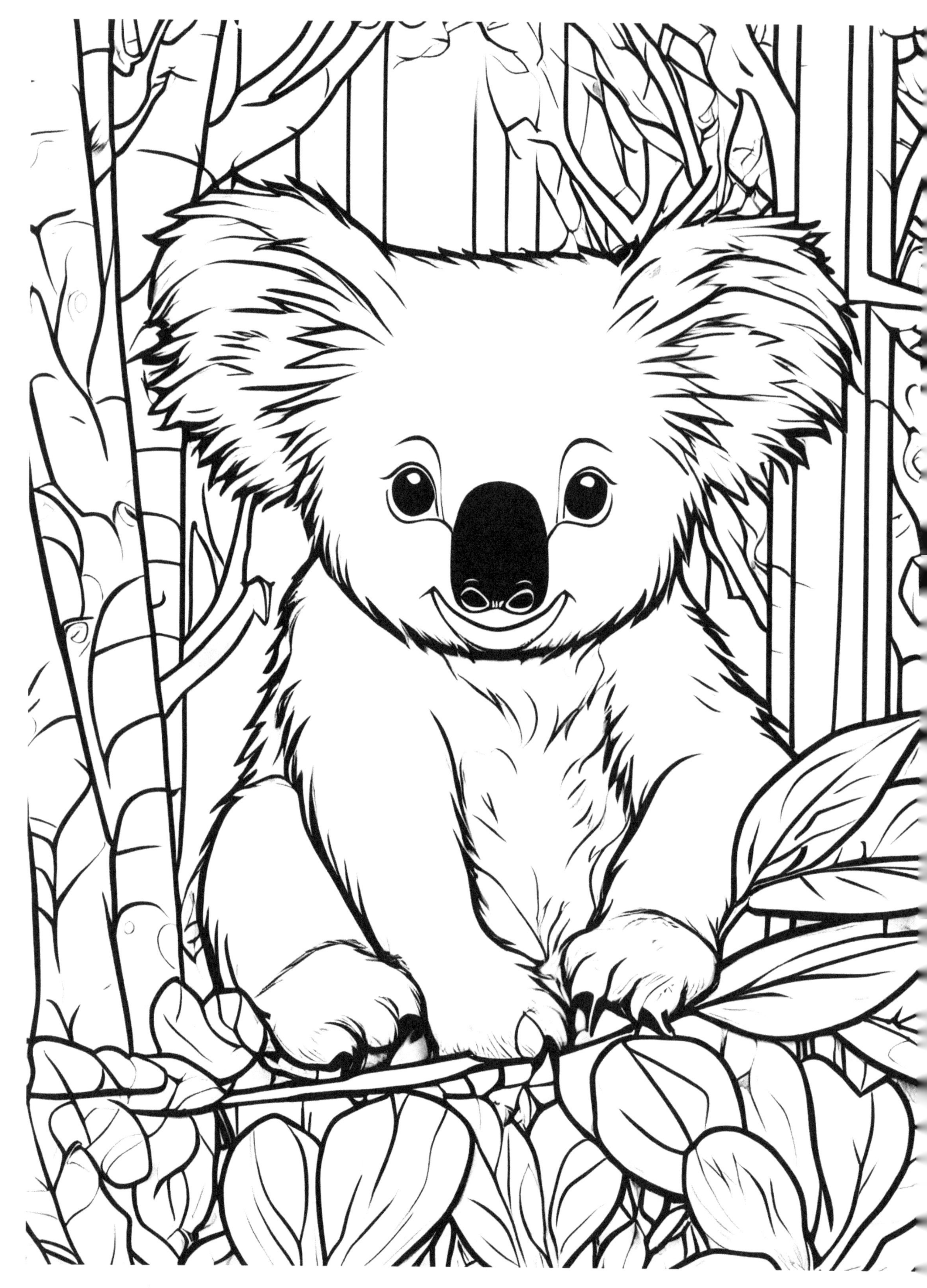

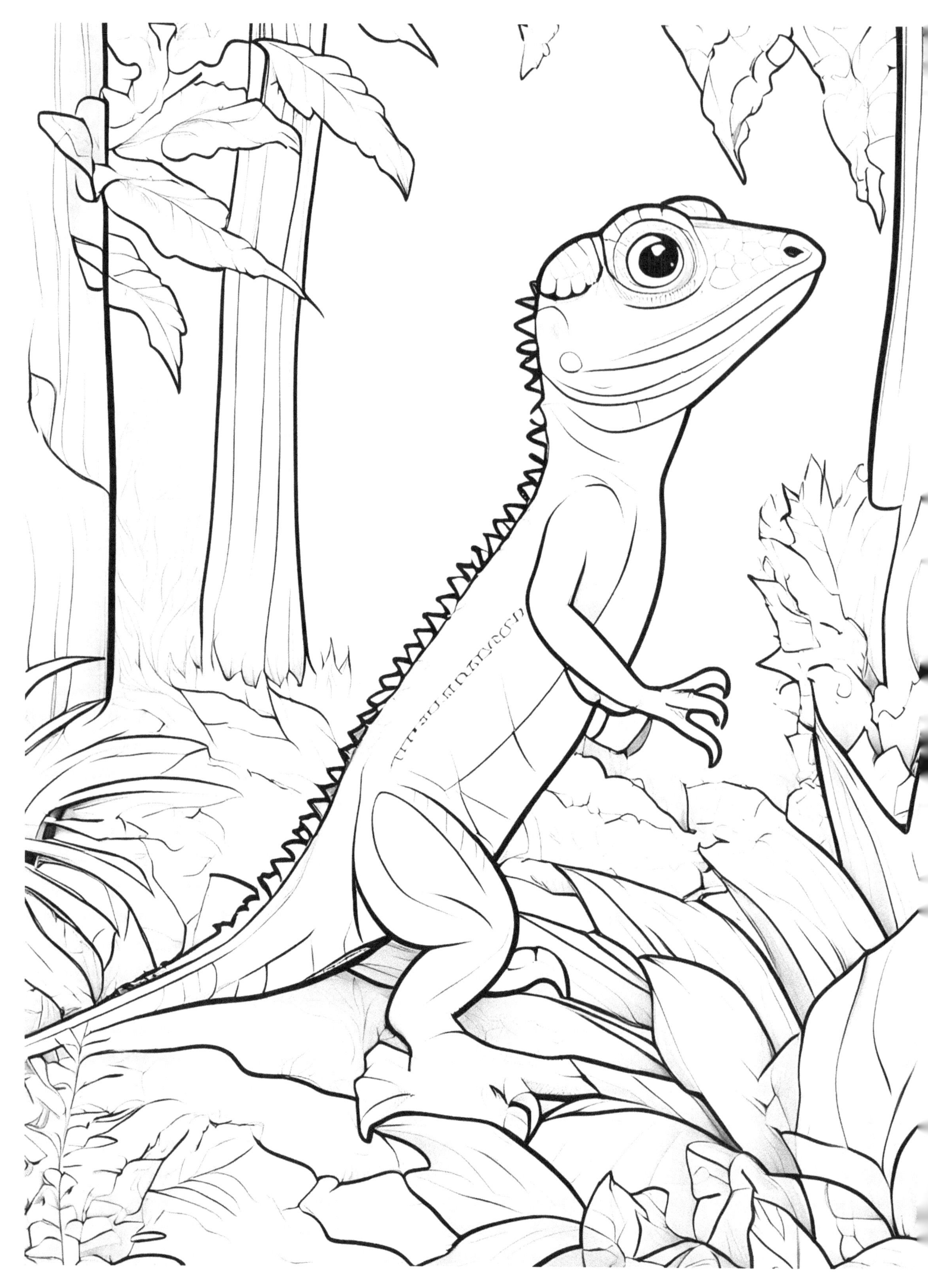

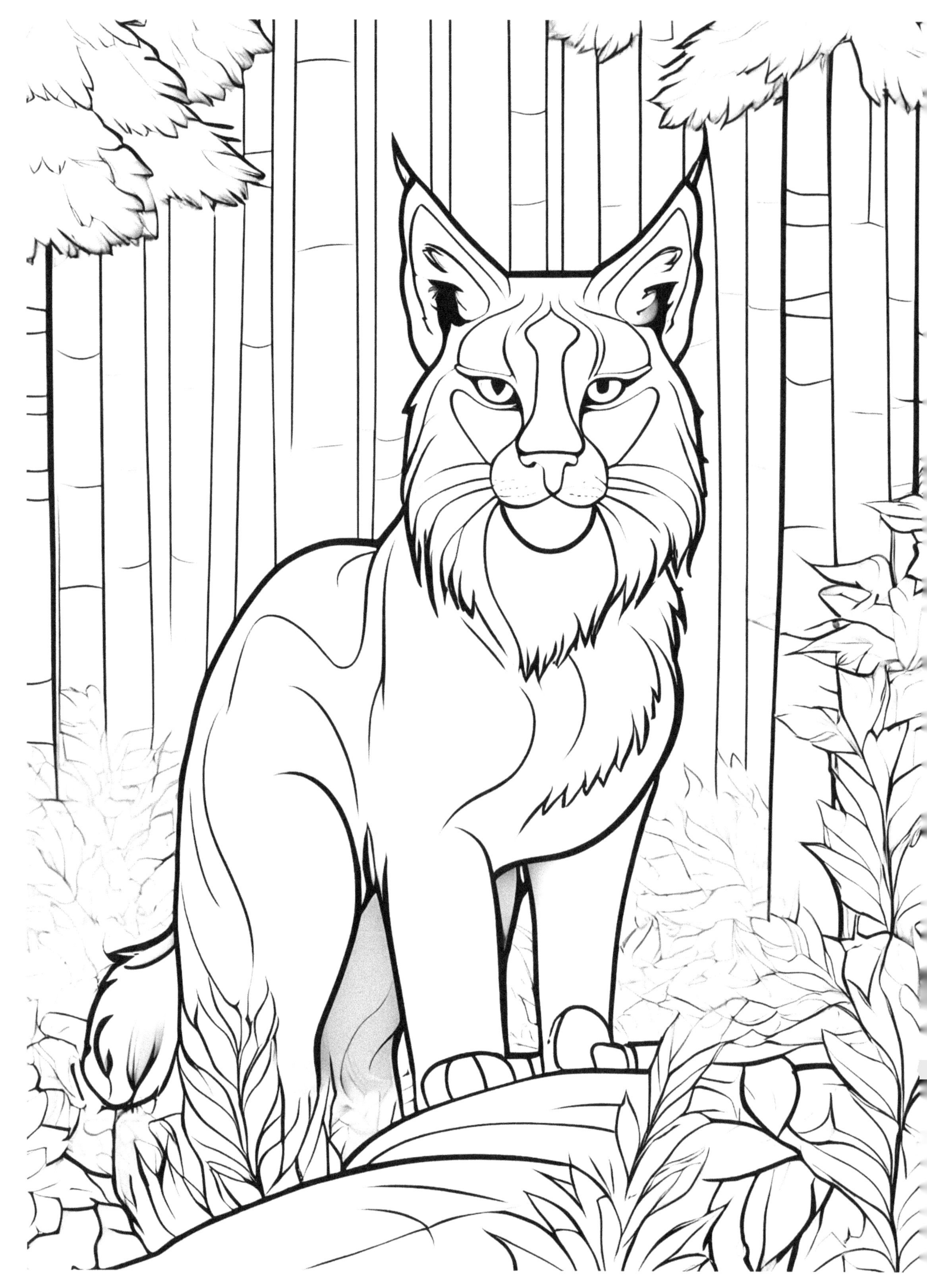

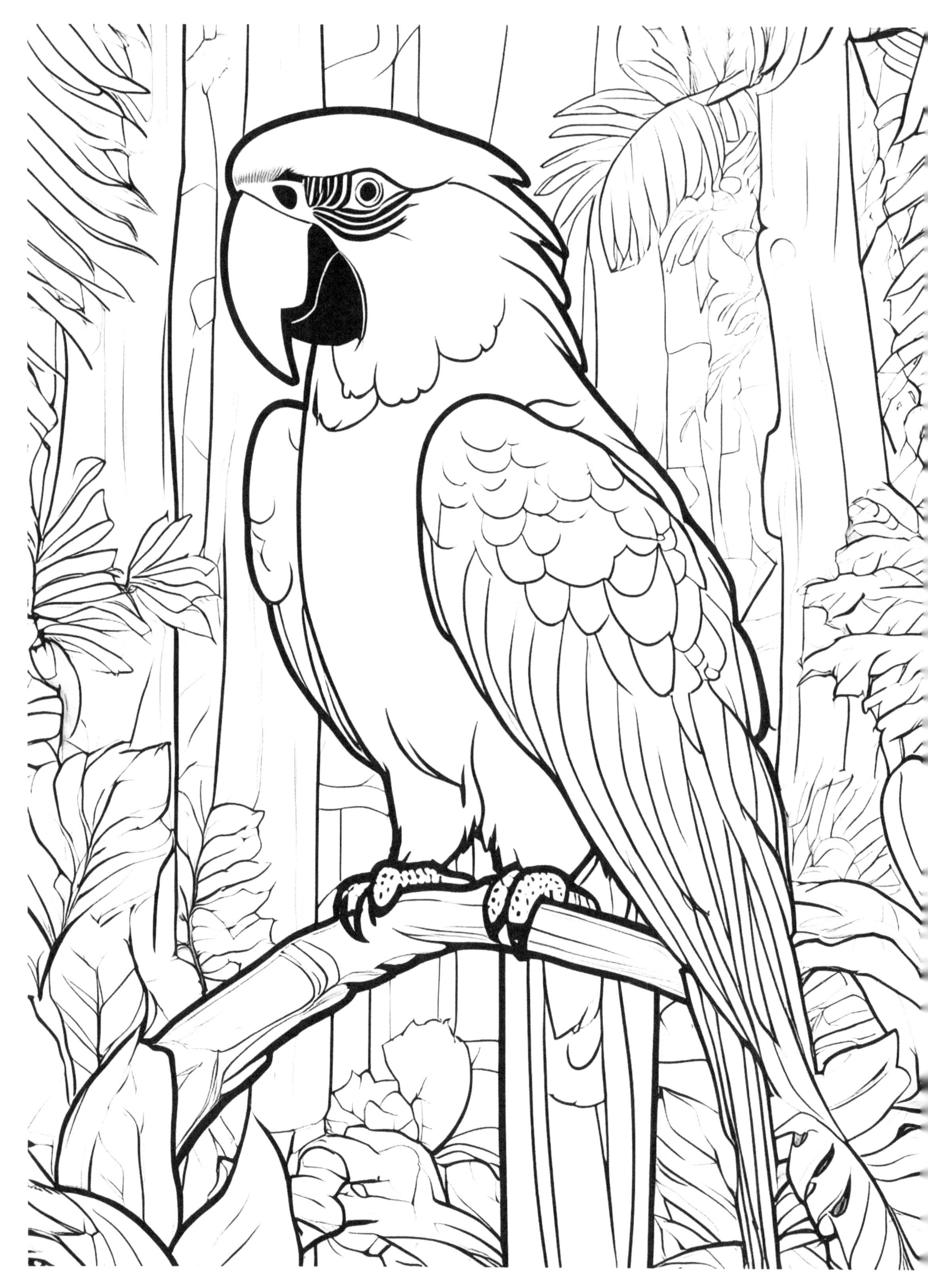

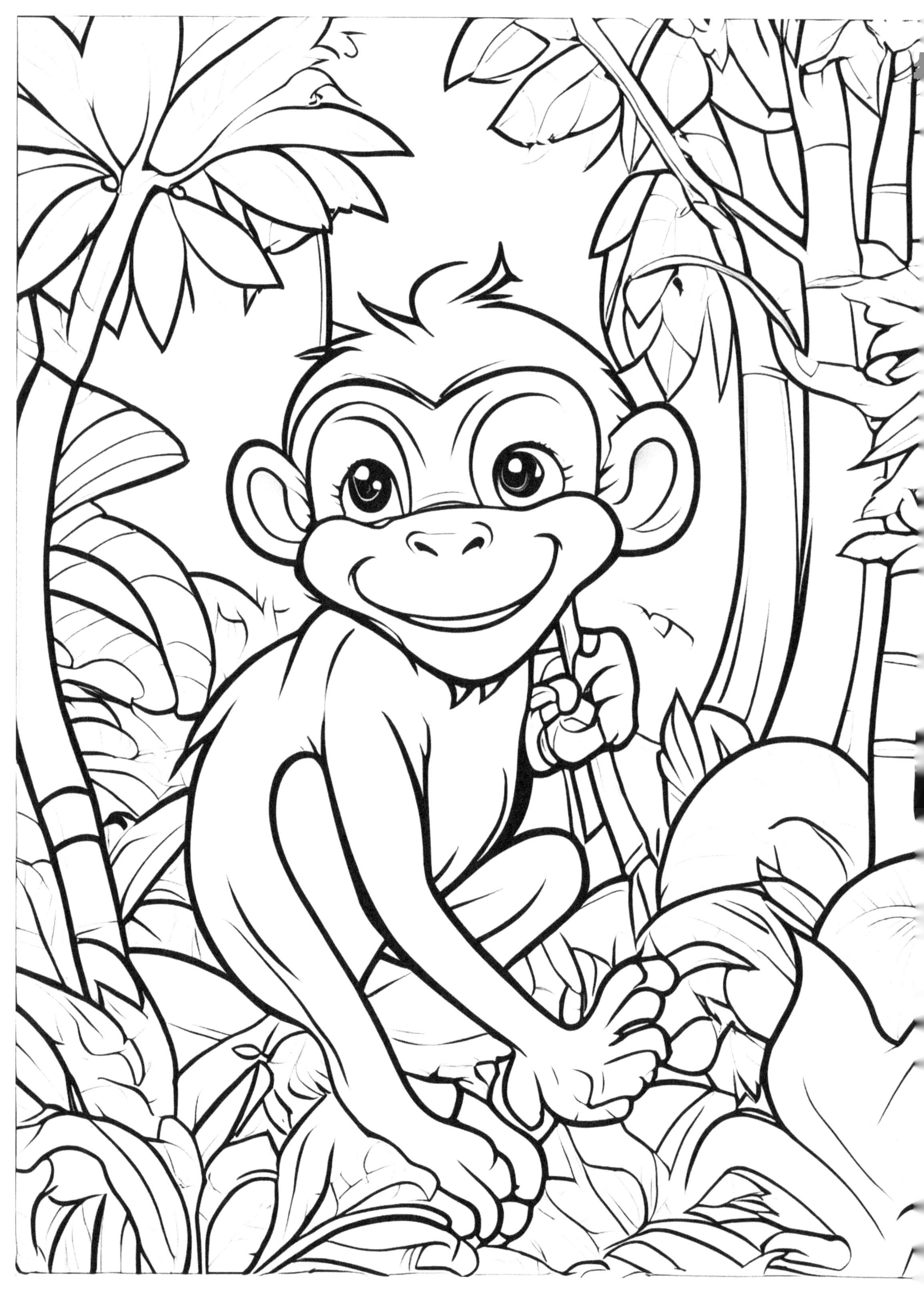

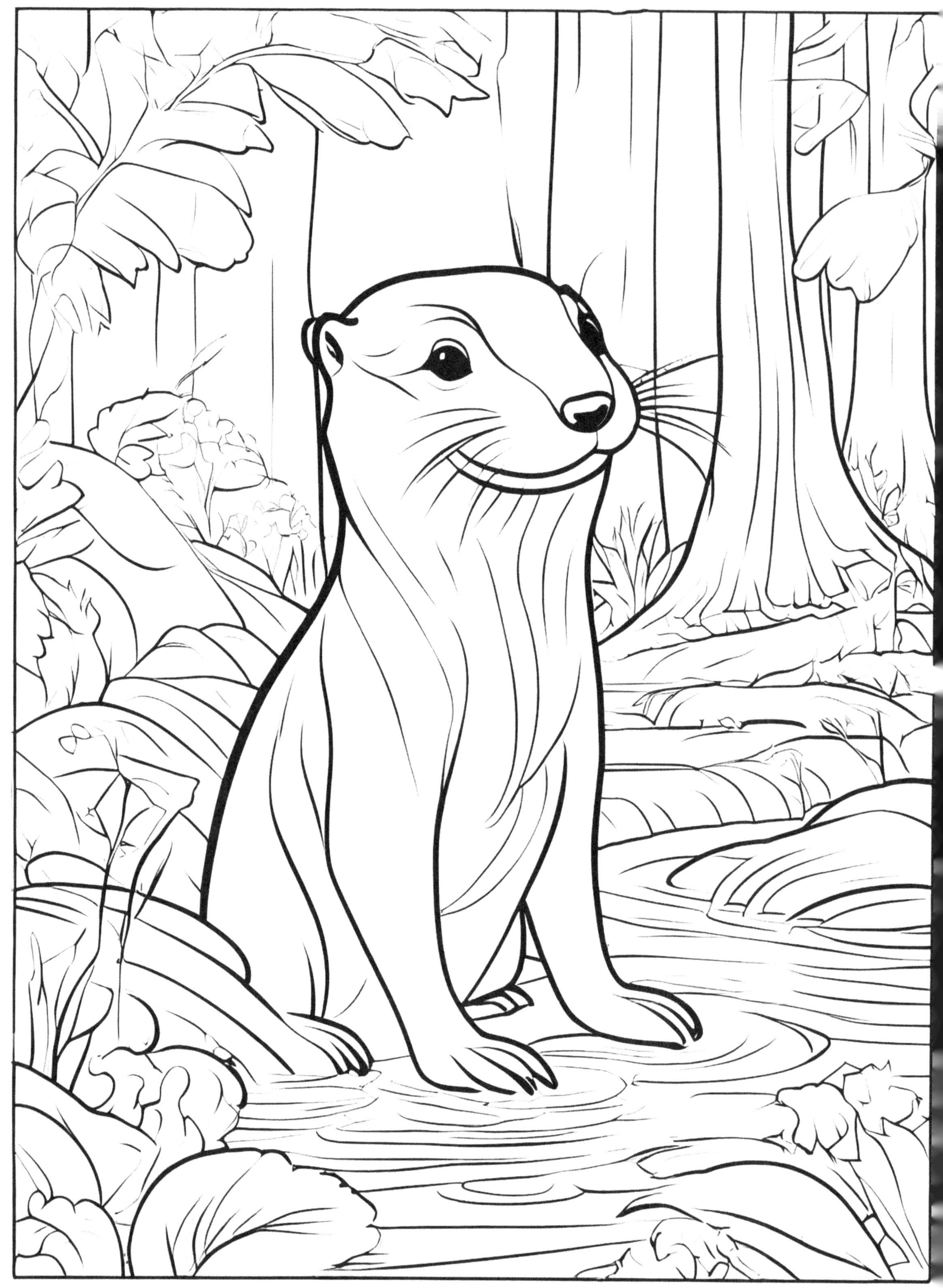

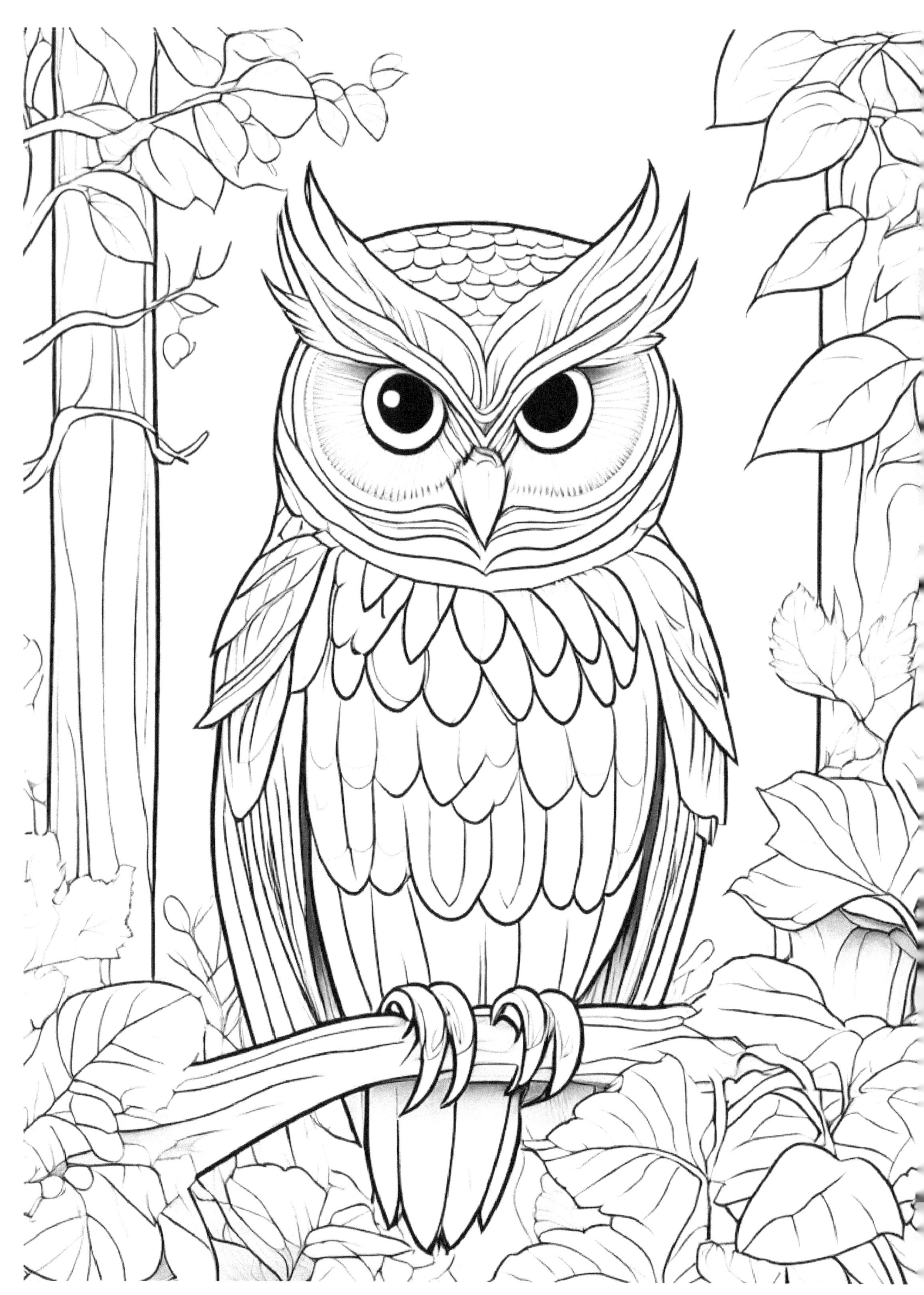

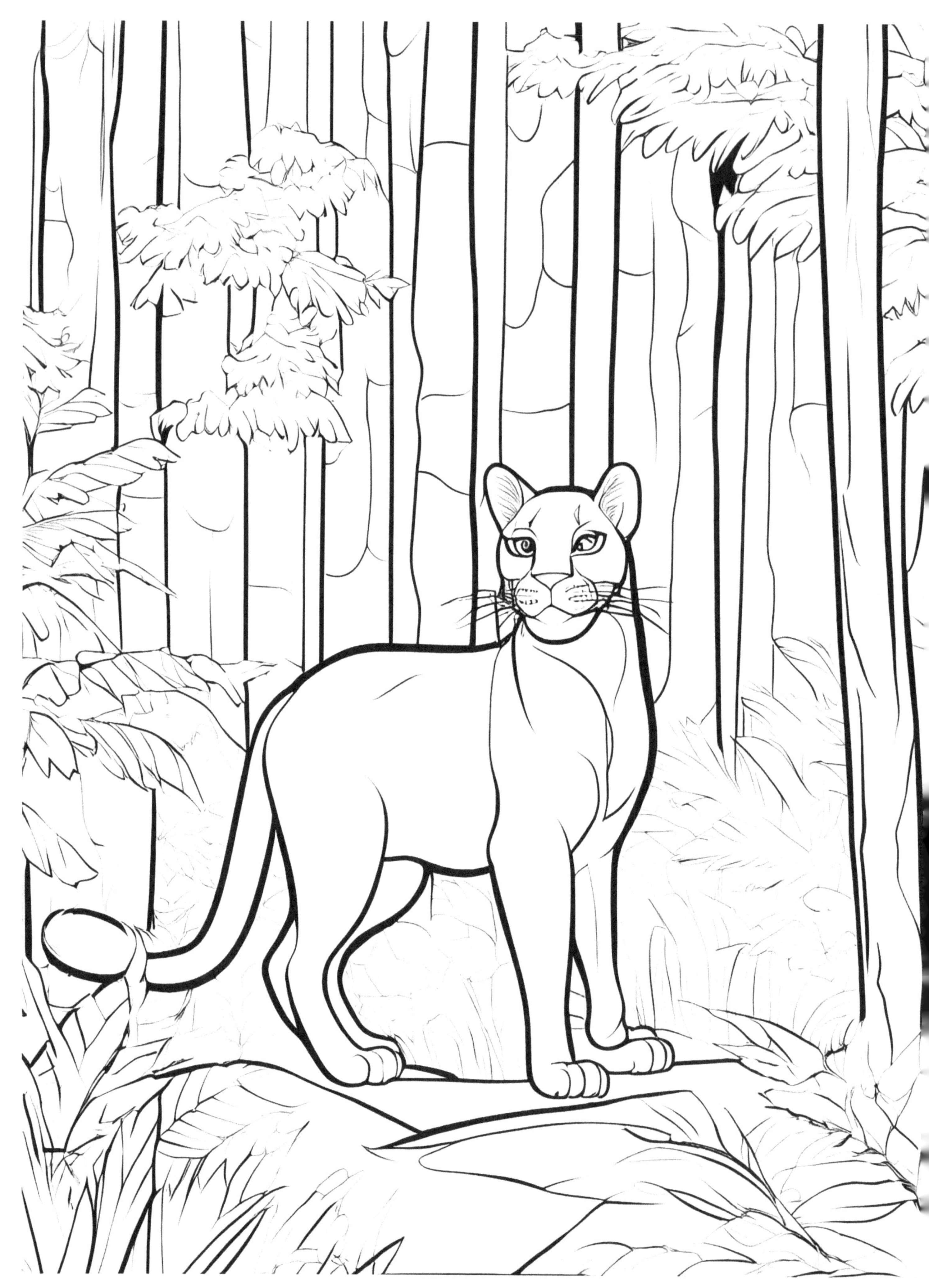

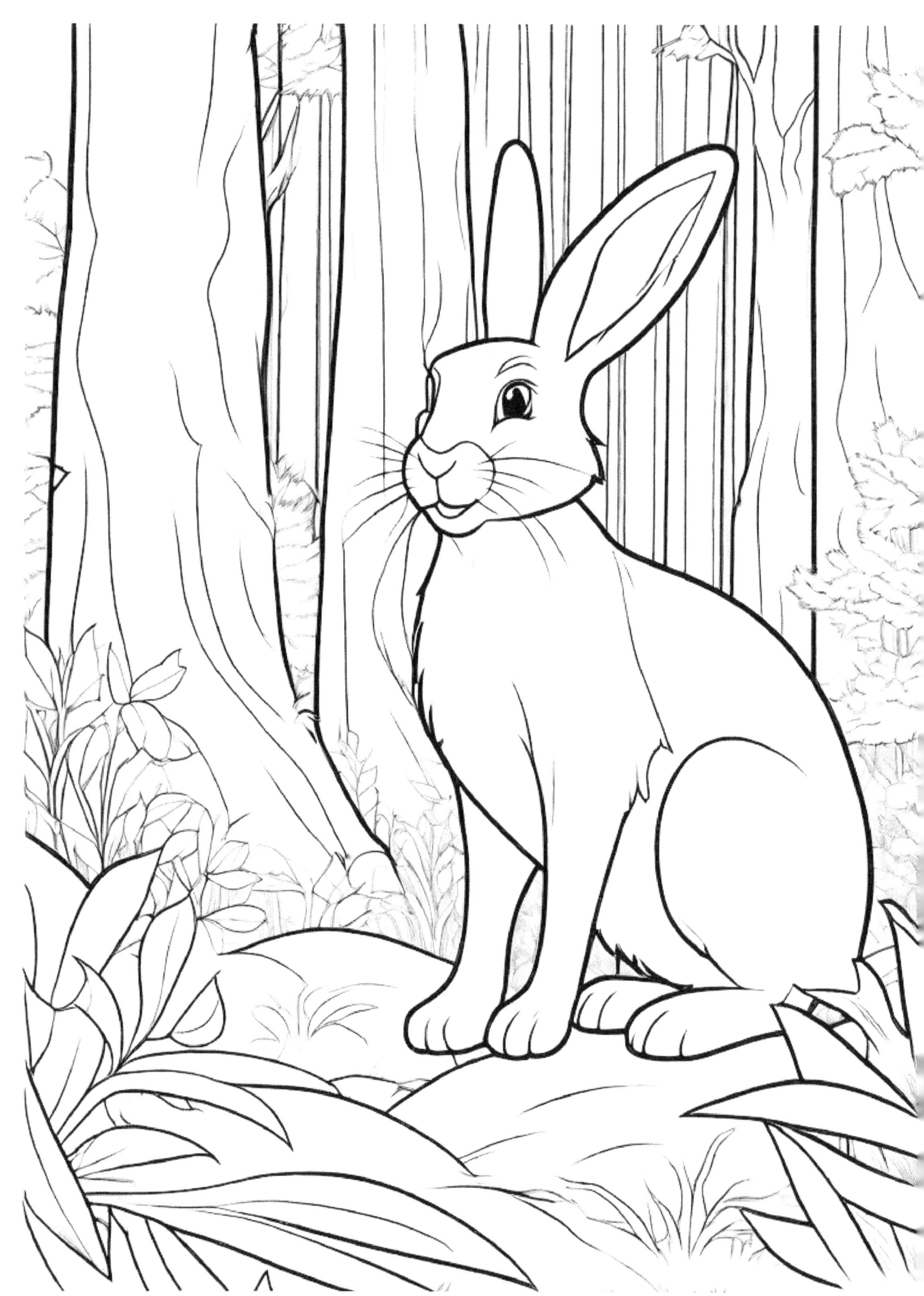

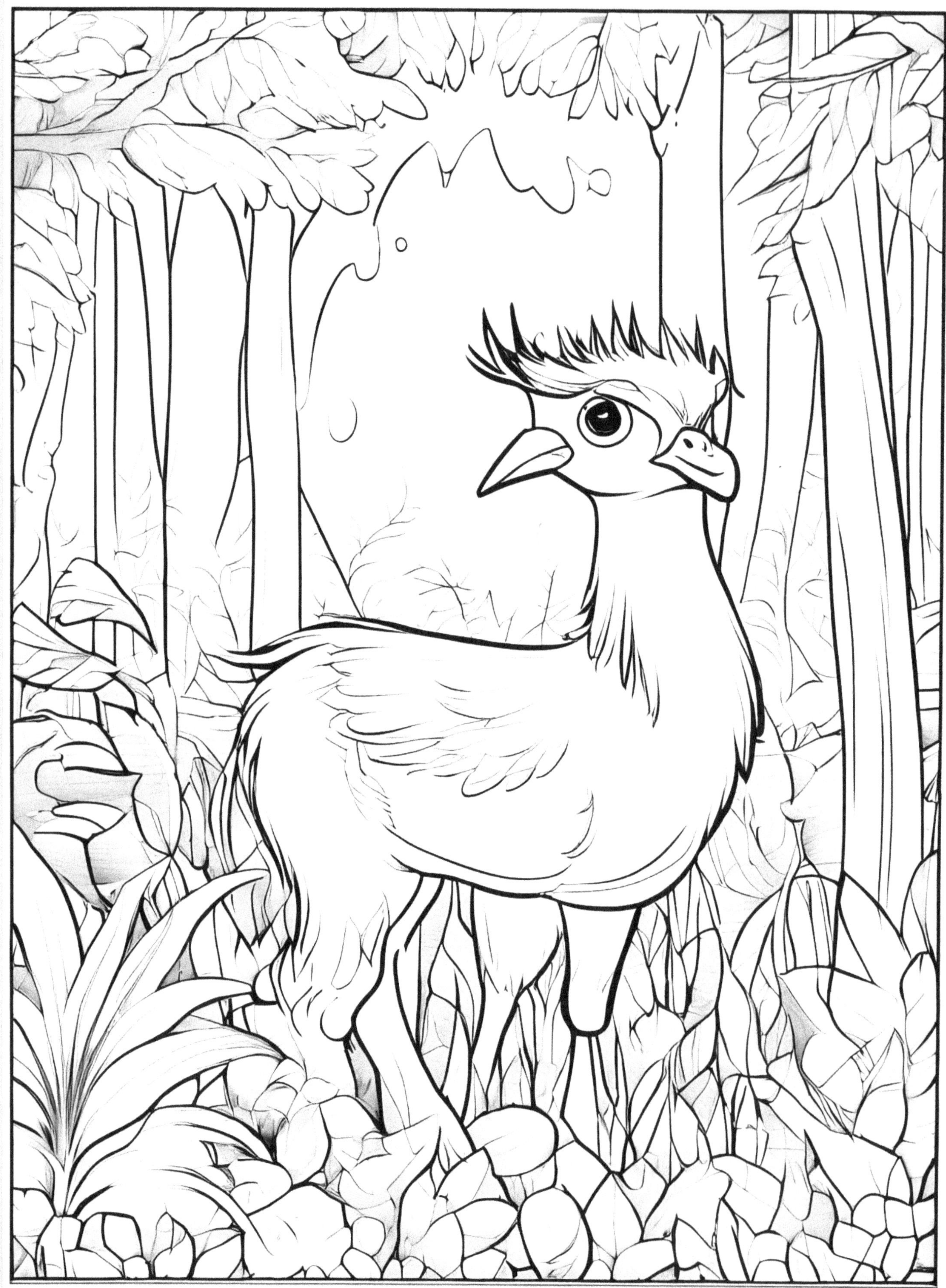

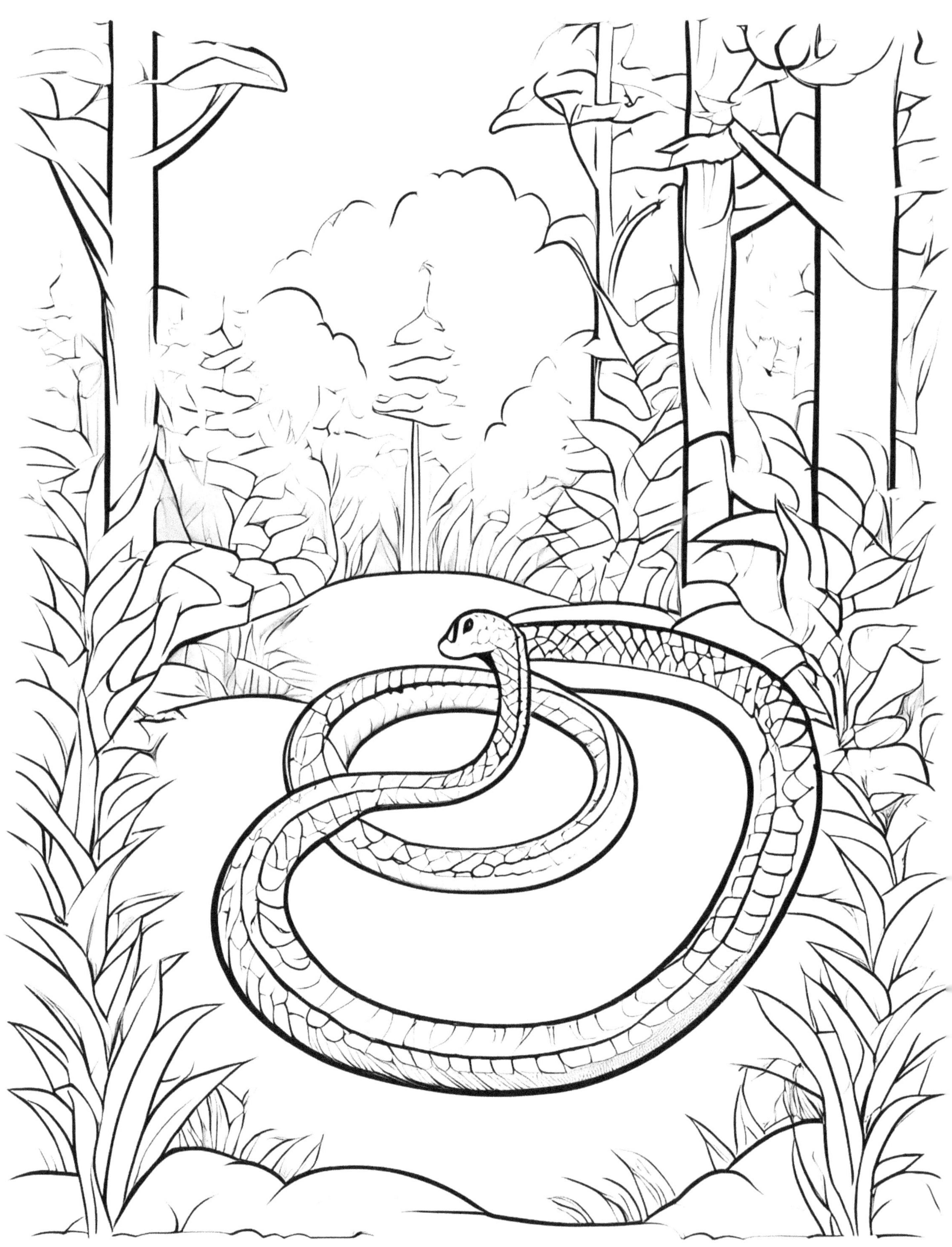

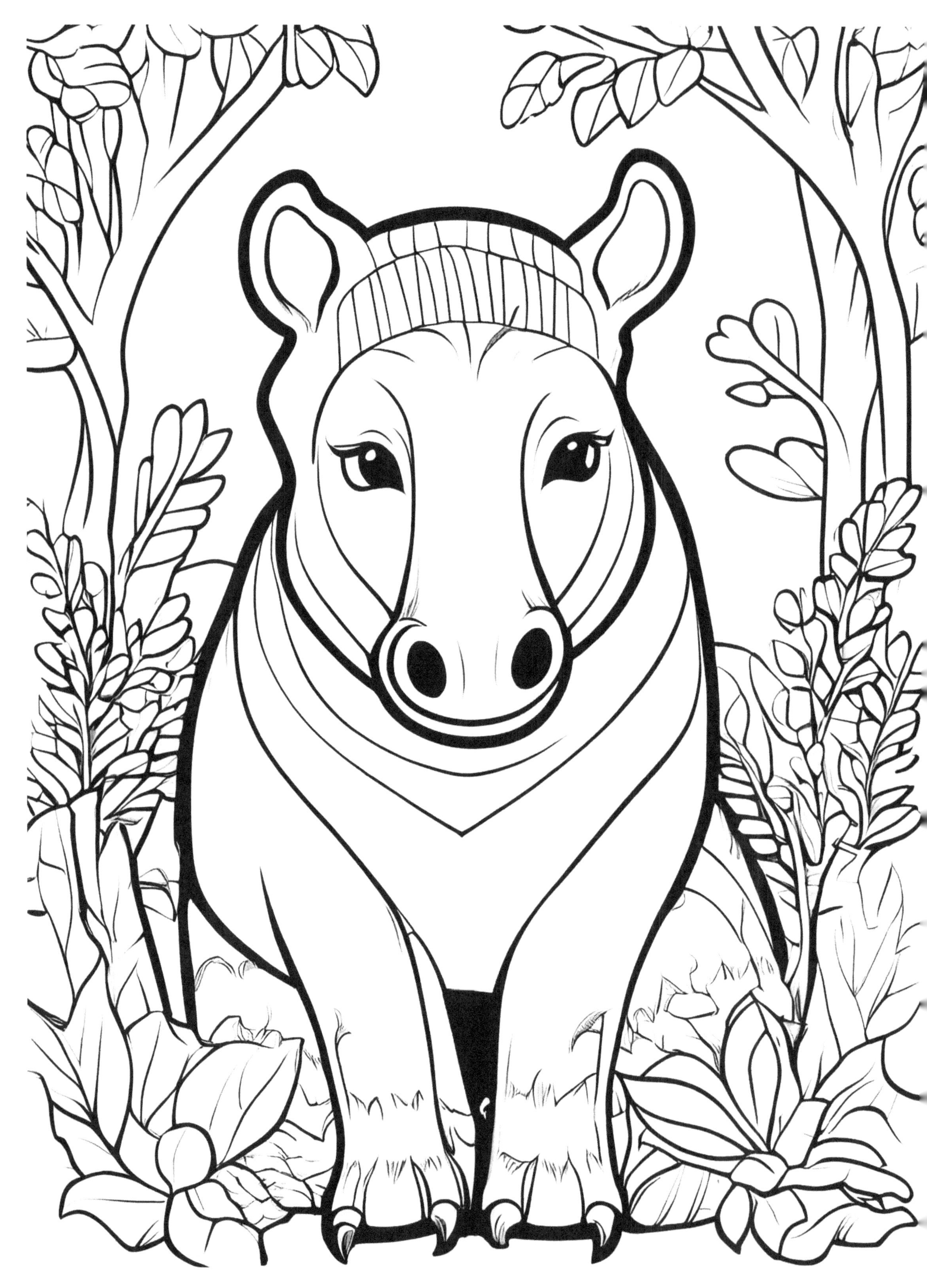

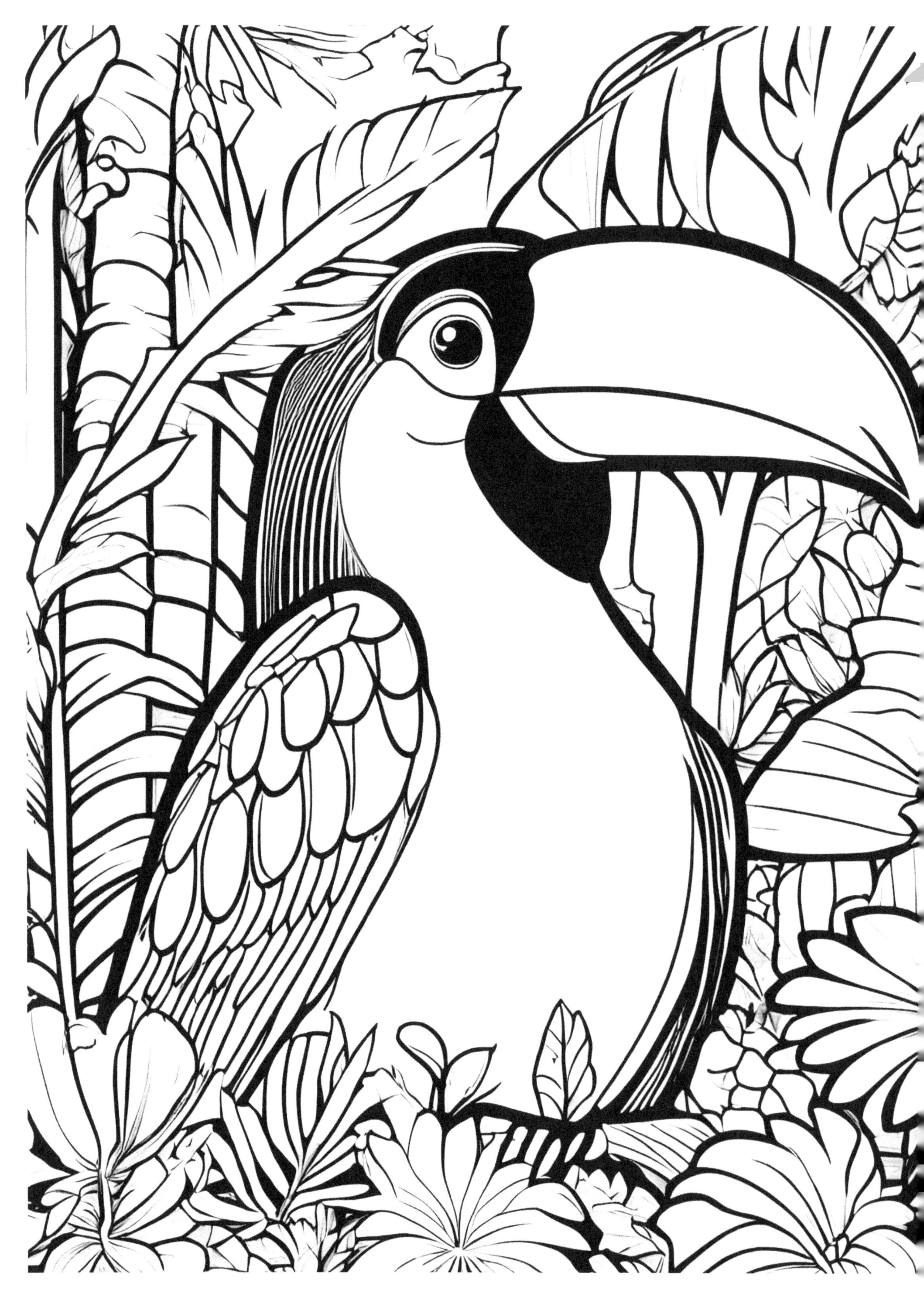

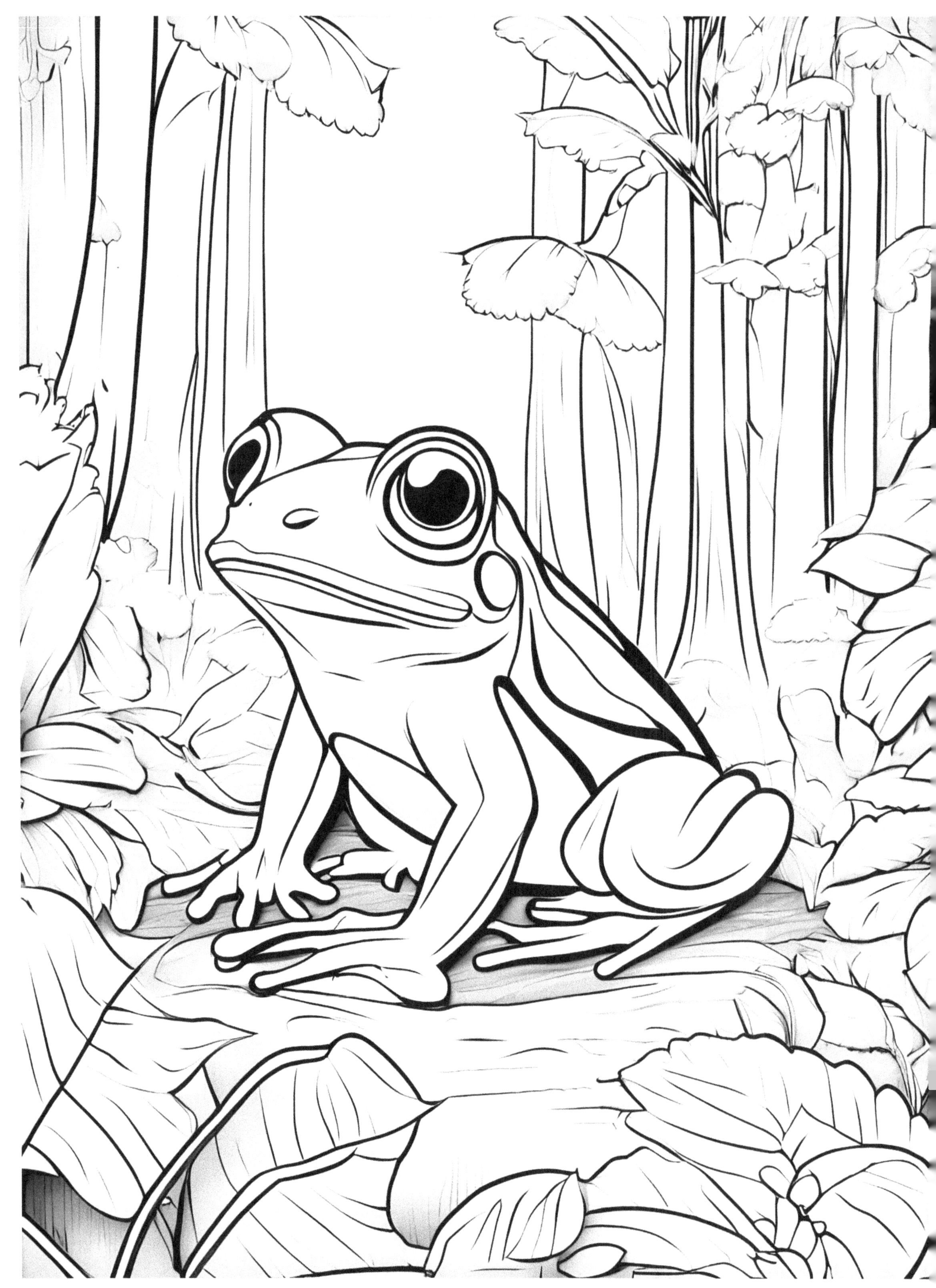

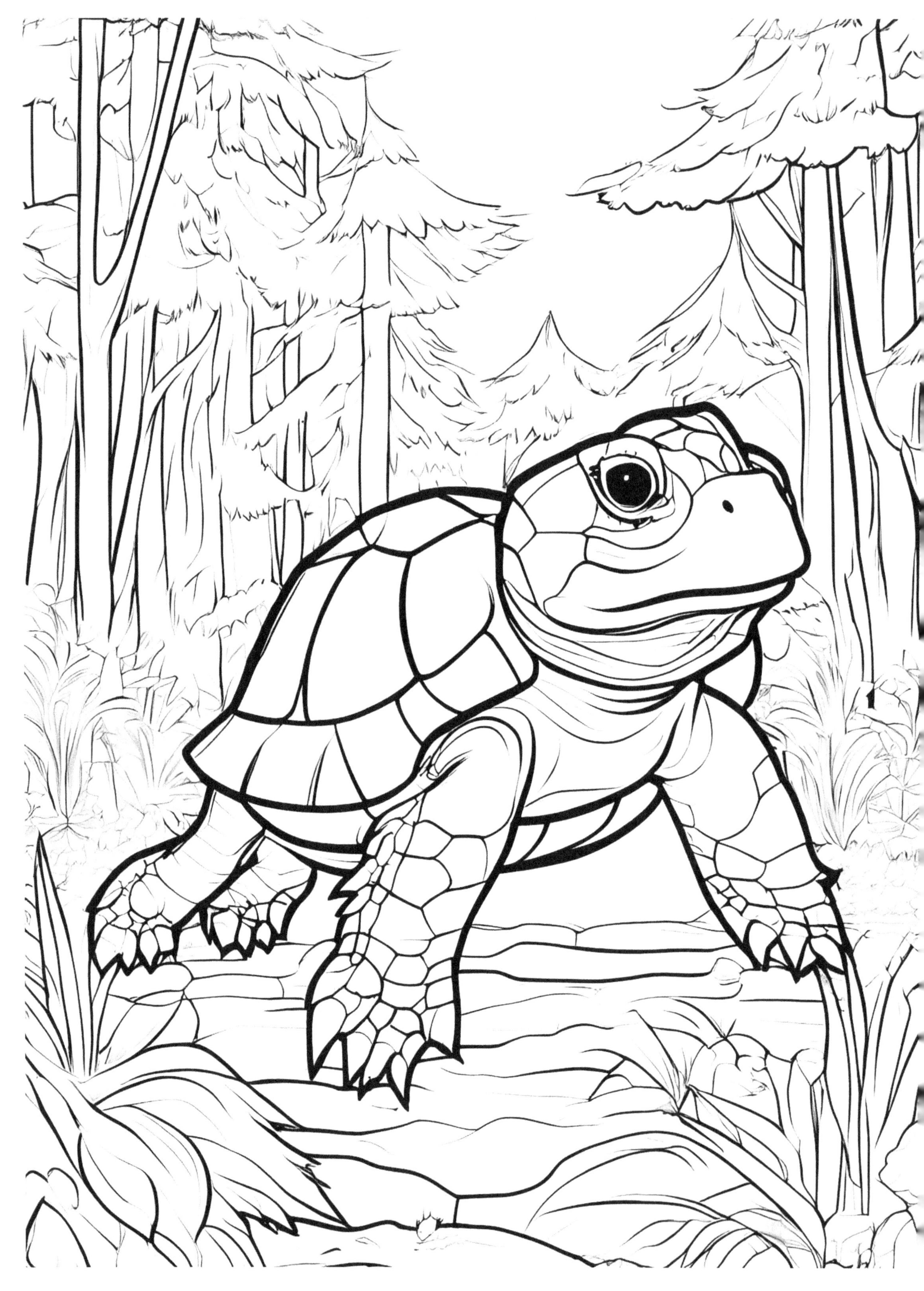

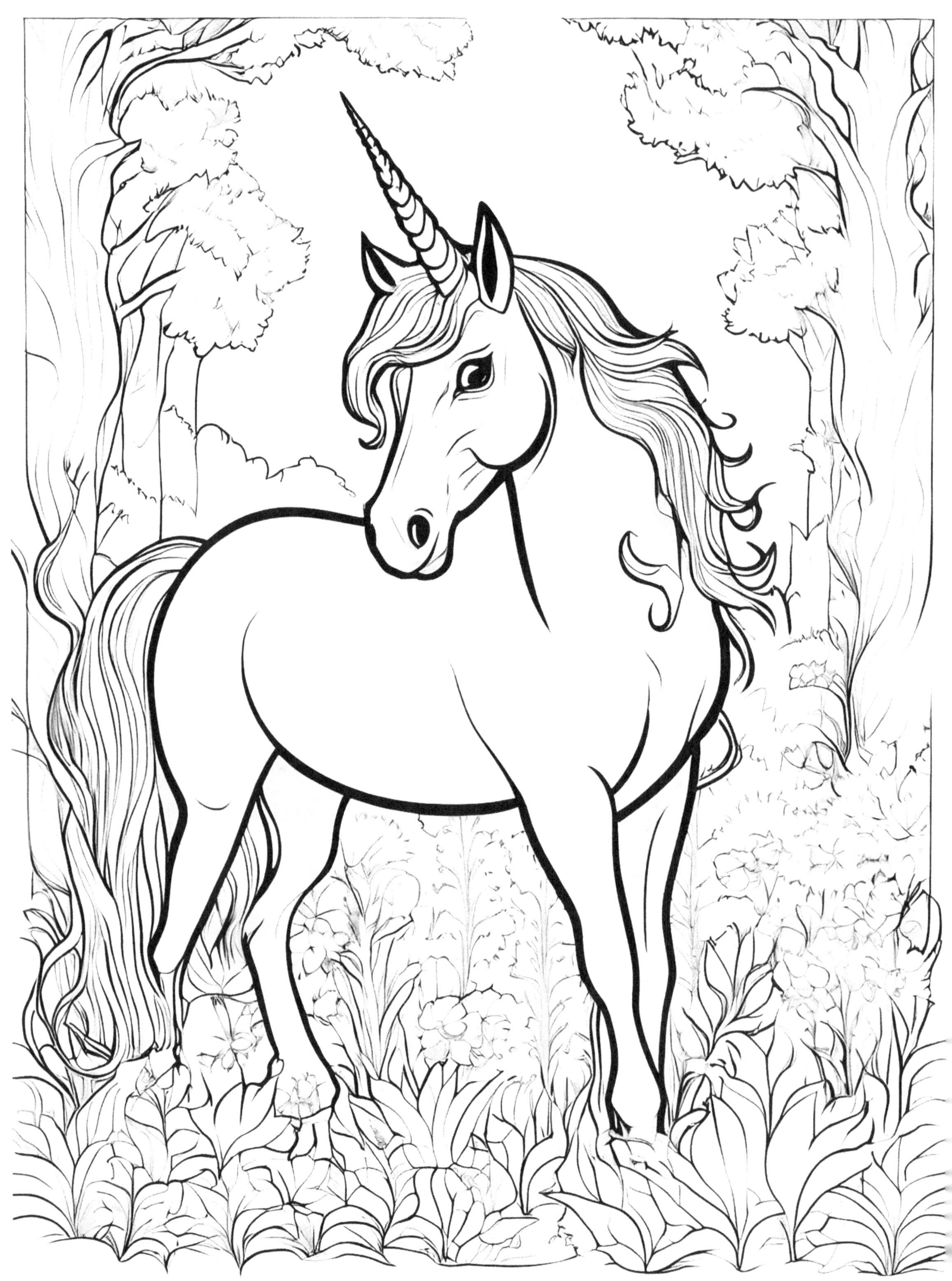

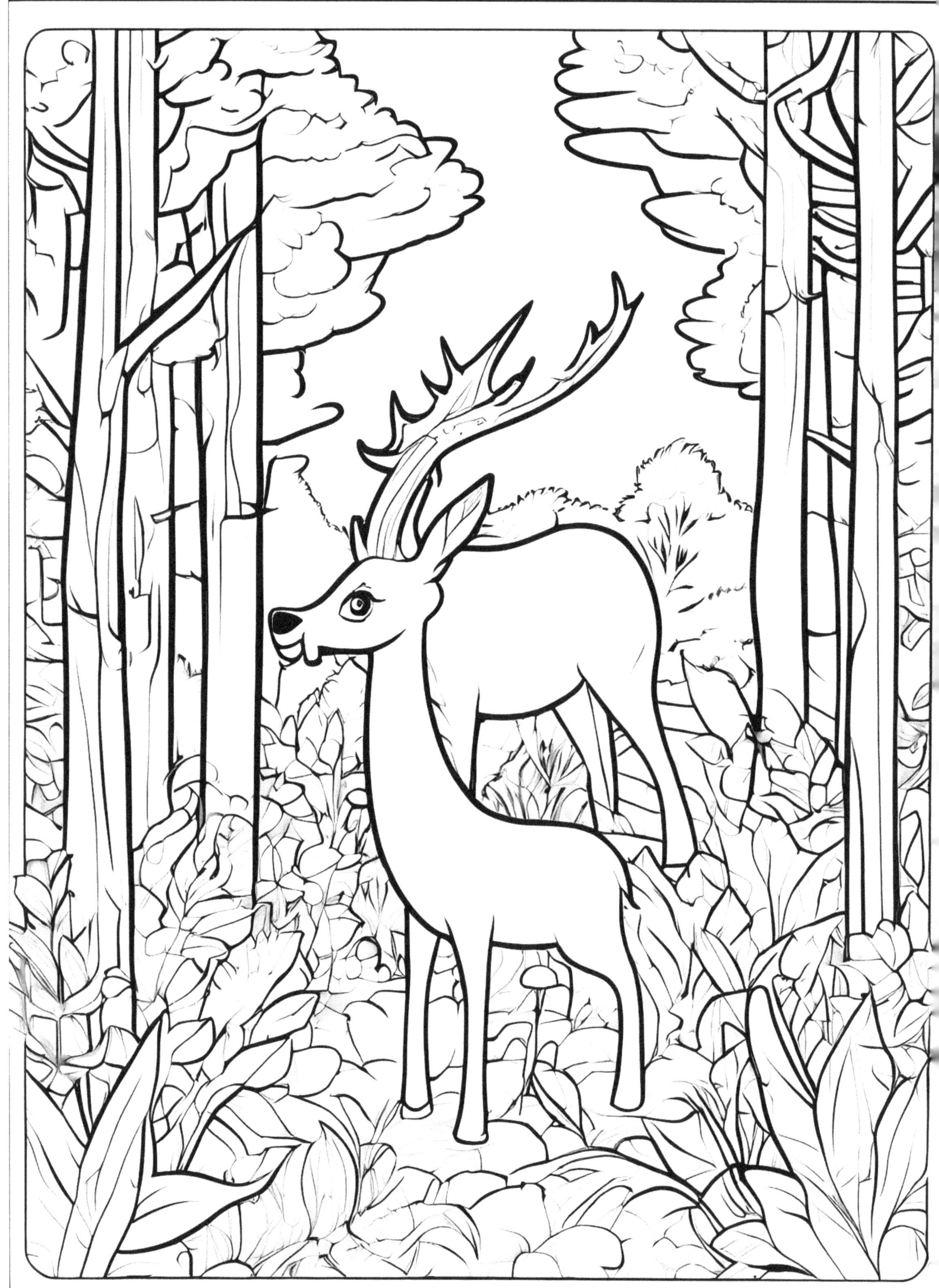